A Different Life

The Strat Goodhue Story

Strat Goodhue

First Call Publishing
Renton, Washington

A Different Life

The Strat Goodhue Story

Cover photo by Strat Goodhue- Ireland, 2018

Library of Congress Control Number: 2018914700

ISBN: 978-0-9858418-6-7

Contents

Introduction

"The unexamined life is not worth living."

- Socrates

Why You Should Read This Book

You may have wondered at times about how rich and famous people got to be where they are. They sometimes have amazing stories of how things lined up for them in such a way that they ended up in "the sweet spot." They were born into a rich family or a relative happened to know someone or they were just in the right place at the right time. Or maybe they were born with or acquired great looks or abilities, or they worked incredibly hard to get to where they are.

But what about me? Why would you want to read a book about my life? I'm not rich or famous. I'm not a superstar. I am just a regular person. But in my journey, I have experienced things that many people only dream about. Some people don't believe these things are real, but I present evidence in this book that will prove that they are real.

This book is about certainty, reality, and things beyond what we see with our eyes. This book may help to confirm some things you may have wondered about. Or you may have thought some of this stuff was ridiculous. But what if it is real? And what if it could change your life?

If you are a skeptic, like I have been my whole life; if you are one of those people who say, "I'll believe it when I see it," then this book may challenge some of your long-held beliefs. Are you willing to be open to learning new things? Are you willing to admit that there may be vast areas of vital truth that you really know little or nothing about?

In this book, I share about some spiritual experiences that many people would find hard or even impossible to believe. But I also share evidence that proves that the spiritual dimension is real, and that what we believe about it, makes a difference; a huge difference, in this life and far beyond this life.

I hope you are not one of those people who say, "I don't care if what I believe is a lie. I only want to believe what I already believe."

This book could help you to know the certainty of spiritual realities that could change your life forever.

1

Bombs and Voices

My mother grew up in a house on Diamond Head in Waikiki. On December 7th, 1941, Pearl Harbor was attacked, and my mother (who was eight years old at the time) along with the rest of her family, looked out their living room window. They could see the black smoke billowing up into the sky from Pearl Harbor. At first, my grandfather thought the smoke was from some practice that might be occurring at Pearl Harbor. But a few minutes later, the phone rang, and the report came to him that Pearl Harbor was being attacked.

My mother's family climbed up onto the roof of their house to watch what was happening. She, along with her brother and sister were counting roofing nails while planes dropped bombs on the ships in Pearl Harbor (or made strafing runs) and then flew up over Diamond Head and made a turn before flying back to Pearl Harbor to drop another bomb, make another strafing run, or fly into the side of a ship. She could see the faces of the Japanese pilots and a few even waved as they flew overhead.

A few days later, my grandfather, who was in the army reserves, was called back into full time military service. He was a successful businessman, but his new job was to try to re-assemble dead soldiers' bodies, so that people could identify and bury those who had been killed in the attack. He knew some of those who had been killed, so this was a very difficult assignment for him.

Prior to the attack, my grandparents hosted parties in their home, which some of the top brass of the military would attend. My mother and her sister would make a game of running up and down their driveway counting stars on the license plates (a sign of rank in the military). (Years later, my grandmother was told (I believe it was by Admiral Nimitz,) that the battle of Iwo Jima was planned on their back porch, drawn out on a cocktail napkin.)

On Christmas night, two and a half weeks after the attack on Pearl Harbor, my grandfather stood up from his chair in the living room, walked upstairs and scolded my mother and her brother for playing with a toy that he had told them not to play with. He then walked back downstairs, sat back down in his chair and died of a heart attack. My mother was eight years old.

My mother asked her mother, "Why did Daddy die?" Her mother gave the best answer she could think of at the time, "God needed him in Heaven more than we needed him on earth?" That was a difficult pill for my mother to swallow. She felt responsible for her father's heart attack, since he had just scolded her for doing something he told her not to do, and then immediately afterwards, had a massive heart attack.

Needless to say, trying to process something like this would be very difficult for an eight-year-old. My mother wasn't sure whether her father died because she had misbehaved or because God was mean and took him away from her. Either way, it didn't sit well with my mother and by the time I knew her as my mother, she had decided that all that "God stuff" was nonsense.

I had somewhat of an unusual childhood even though it probably appeared normal to a lot of people. I was born and raised in Hawai'i. My parents were divorced when I was five years old. My three sisters and I lived with my mother and on Sundays, my father would pick us up and take us for the day. Usually, part of that day involved taking us to what I would now call, a "dead church." It had a form of religion but there didn't seem to be any real "life" in the church (at least that's how I perceived it). And it was very boring. The pastor had a drinking problem and his son had a drug problem. It seemed very routine to me- sort of like people going through the motions but not really believing what they said they believed. It seemed like useless religion.

My father would bring us home after the dead religious church services on Sundays and my mother would then tell us kids that all that God stuff was nonsense. What she said made sense to me so decided I was an atheist. There must not be a God.

A Skeptic on a Spiritual Journey

My atheistic beliefs allowed for some spiritual realities, however, since I had started having "out-of-body experiences" when I was four years old. (An "out-of-body experience" is an experience in which a person's soul or spirit apparently leaves their body. It's also known as "astral projection.") At first, these events only occurred when I was sleeping. The experiences were like dreams except they were much more vivid, and I had some control of myself in these "dreams." After my first out-of-body experience, I didn't have another one for a year or so. Then I started having them several times a year. As time went by, I learned the technique of being able to control myself in these experiences, or as I in time came to describe it, I learned how to "direct my will."

Being able to rise up off my bed and to fly, was exhilarating to say the least. As I will share in a little bit, I eventually received some very convincing evidence to support the idea that these were not just dreams, they were actual out-of-body experiences. More on this a bit later in my testimony.

A Running Stop

Another childhood experience that made me think about the reality of the spiritual realm was when I was attending a summer youth program at the YMCA in Kailua, a few miles from where I lived. I was about 11 years old.

Every day, we had a little free time. On several occasions, a few of us kids walked out onto a heiau (ancient Hawai'ian place of worship and sacrifice, pronounced "hay-eeow") that was located directly next to the YMCA. The heiau was a large, mostly flat area made up of lava rocks. We would venture out onto the heiau to explore the area and play. One day, I started picking up some rocks and throwing them and some other kids joined in. We didn't know enough to realize that this was an archeological site and a place that would be considered sacred to many Hawai'ian people.

When the break time ended, and the call was made to go back into the YMCA, I was standing near the center of the heiau. I started to walk back toward the YMCA and as I walked, I involuntarily started running. The thought occurred to me, "Why am I running?" I hadn't even thought of running. I just found myself sprinting across the rocks, running toward the edge of the heiau. As I got within a few feet of the boundary of the heiau, I tripped and fell, spraining both of my wrists quite severely.

I had never in my life started to run without intending to run. It was a very strange experience. Immediately after I had been throwing rocks in a sacred Hawai'ian place, I started running fast without any intention on my part whatsoever, and then tripped and sprained both my wrists. It wasn't a life-changing experience for me, but it did make me think. Could Hawai'ian spirits be real? Could they have compelled me to run and then trip me, in order to teach me a lesson? Something sure seemed to have made me do it. It made me wonder, but my mind quickly went on to other things that kids think about.

A Message from Beyond

When I was in intermediate school, I had an experience that opened my eyes to a whole new realm of spiritual reality. First, a little background to this experience. My oldest sister, Brooksie, had an experience one night as she lay in bed. She said she awoke from her sleep and opened her eyes and sitting at the foot of her bed, was an elderly Hawai'ian woman. My sister insisted that this was not a dream. She said she closed her eyes tightly for a bit, opened them up again and the woman was still there. She closed her eyes again and held them closed for what seemed like a long time. She opened her eyes again and the woman was gone.

The only way in or out of my sister's bedroom was through a set of old sliding wooden Japanese "shoji" doors that had some very squeaky wheels. There would be no way for someone to go in or out of the room without making noise. But my sister insisted that it was not a dream- she was wide awake, and the woman was in her room and then was gone.

My sister went off to college a few months later and that room became my bedroom. One night, after several months of it being my room, I noticed something strange. I had no problem sleeping in the room but one night as I was going to lay down and read on the bed, I felt a strong tension in my upper abdomen. I called our three dogs into the room and they came in, circled around and walked out of the room. I tried to get them to lay down in the room, but they did not want to do that.

I mentioned that experience to my mother and she said she would talk with Rudy, the park historian at

Waimea Falls Park, where she worked. (Rudy was knowledgeable about Hawai'ian spirituality). He asked my mother for a key to the house and said that sometime in the next two weeks, he would visit the house and see if there was a spirit living in the house with us.

I didn't think much about it but a few days later, I was at school during the lunch break and I was standing against a railing and suddenly, a Hawai'ian word popped into my head- "Makua." I didn't know what the word meant or where it came from. It was just suddenly in my mind. Being raised in Hawai'i, I probably knew about 50 words in the Hawai'ian language and at the time, the Hawai'ian language was not commonly spoken in public (other than a few dozen words).

A few days later, I was standing next to the telephone in our kitchen when another Hawai'ian word started to pop into my mind. This time, I had to speak the first syllable of the word out loud and worked to add a syllable at a time until it felt right- "Om, ome, omi, omau..." The second word- "omauka." Again, I didn't know what the word meant. I wrote it down along with the first word that had come to me a few days earlier. I grabbed a Hawai'ian-English dictionary off the shelf and looked up the two words.

Makua o'mauka. The definition- "Old, respected person, with motion towards the mountains." That didn't mean anything to me so when my mother came home from work that evening, I asked her if she could ask the Rudy what had happened. She came back from work the next day with an interesting report. She said Rudy told her that he had come into the house spiritually, not physically, and that he found a spirit of an elderly Hawai'ian woman there. He said that he told the spirit that she didn't need to stay in the house, that she could go to Waimea valley (the valley is in a mountainous area) where there were many other spirits.

He said she then left our house and went to Waimea valley.

You might not believe that there are any spiritual realities. You might think that people's "spiritual experiences" are just peoples' imaginations going wild. But you must admit that someone being told something in a foreign language, something they don't understand until it's translated, that describes an event that they didn't know had happened, and then finding out later that the event that was described to them, had (reportedly) occurred, is noteworthy in regard to the possible existence of a spiritual dimension.

I tend to be a skeptic. I am a fairly analytical kind of a "prove it" type of person. So even though I was an atheist, I had to admit that these experiences seemed to be evidence of a dimension of reality that I (at one point) really didn't think existed.

And these spiritual experiences were just the beginning.

2

Out of My Body and Awake!

By the time I was in high school, I was having out-of-body experiences every two or three months. The thrill of flying was exhilarating. I wished I could have them more often.

Leif, a friend of mine who had a jeep that was outfitted for off-road driving, along with my younger sister Shaun, and a few friends and I would go off-roading at a place called "banana patch." It was near the base of the Pali (the Hawai'ian word for "cliff") on the windward side of O'ahu.

One night as we were having fun off-roading, we happened to drive up to the top end of a big open field. At the end of this field, there was a band of rainforest that ran along the base of the Pali. Leif stopped the Jeep and I got out and walked a few feet into the forest. As a joke, Leif and the rest of the crew took off in the Jeep, leaving me alone in the dark. I heard the noise of the Jeep getting quieter as they drove off. I knew their departure was a joke and that they would soon return.

I wasn't thinking much of anything as I walked into the forest. But as I walked a little further into the forest, I noticed the sounds of twigs and branches breaking. A snap here and a snap there. There was no wind that night, so it was very still. It occurred to me that these noises were too loud to be coming from leaves or twigs falling off the trees. I thought they must be coming from wild pigs in the forest. Wild boars in Hawai'i are usually very afraid of people, but they can be quite dangerous, or at least that is what was going through my mind at the time. I thought, "What if there are some boars that have piglets and they think I am a threat? They could charge me and maybe even kill me."

Maybe this was an irrational fear, but at the time, it was very real to me. I thought I could possibly be seriously injured or even killed. I then figured, "If I am going to die, I am going to die. My fear is not going to make any difference. I need to overcome my fear." I stepped further into the forest in order to confront my fear head on.

In order to make myself as vulnerable as possible (in order to fully face my fear), I stepped into the center of a clearing in the forest. I figured while I couldn't see them (because of the darkness), the boars could probably see me, and could attack me if they wanted too. It was very dark. As I stood there, I realized how quiet the night was. It was very still other than the sounds of the twigs and branches breaking.

As I stood there in the middle of that clearing in the forest, I became more and more motionless. I stopped my slight swaying back and forth and within a short period of time, my senses became much more heightened. I could feel the temperature of the skin on the outside of my body, but I was also aware of the inside my body.

Within a few minutes, I felt like I was starting to rise up out of my body. It felt like I hovered about 12 feet above the ground for about 10 minutes. While I was floating up there, I could see the same things I could see when I was in my body, but it was from a higher vantage point. It then felt like I slowly drifted back down into my body. It was an amazing experience. I realize that I have no evidence that I can present to you that would prove that my spirit or soul was outside of my body, but I share it because it was quite an experience for me. I had been having out-of-body experiences over a period of 10+ years in my sleep, and this was one of only two out-of-body experiences that I had while I was awake. (I believe I levitated once when I was about eight years old, from a sitting position on the floor in my bedroom.)

The experience was amazing. I had a wonderful sense of peace and was completely calm when my friends and sister came rumbling back up the field in the Jeep.

An Education

I attended a public high school and of course, was taught Darwin's theory of evolution. It made perfect sense to me and I had never heard any reasonable challenges to the theory, so I assumed it was true. Like many Americans, I thought someone would have to be an idiot to not believe in the theory of evolution. While I was comfortable with the idea of evolution, the logical conclusion I came to as a result of my belief in evolution was troubling.

Of course, Darwin's theory teaches that we (human beings) are just a result of billions of random accidental events occurring over a period of hundreds of millions of years on a rock (earth) that just happened to be the perfect distance from the sun to have an environment that is favorable to life. And maybe, a lightning bolt just happened to hit a puddle of muddy water (or something like that), that just happened to be on this rock. And it somehow just happened to produce the first single celled organism.

In fact, Prokaryote bacteria are considered to be the first single-cell animals, claimed to have been found among the oldest known rocks on Earth (supposedly 3.5B years old). However, when closely studied with electron computer imaging, they found this "earliest" tiny creature amazingly complex, made with many millions of molecules operating in perfect order- similar to the complexity of a Boeing 747! (But with seven motors, not four, like a 747.)

Believing that this could happen by random chance is like believing that a tornado blowing through a junkyard could produce a perfectly functioning 747 (that can repair itself and reproduce itself). It takes a lot of faith to believe in a theory like that.

Personally, I don't believe that a tornado blowing through a junkyard could produce a 747. I don't believe a tornado could produce a Porsche, or even a Pop-Tart, especially one that could repair itself and reproduce itself.

You get the idea- according to Darwinian evolution, the existence of humankind is just a result of billions of amazingly freak coincidences in a bizarre chain of cosmic accidents. (For more information about evolution, check out: www.answersingenesis.org)

It seems to me that it takes a tremendous amount of blind faith to believe that living cells (which are amazingly complex) somehow developed by random chance from non-living chemicals. And that these cells also developed with the ability to write, read and interpret the incredibly complex code of DNA (which instructs the cells how to function, how to duplicate themselves and even to repair themselves).

Charles Darwin wrote in his book, Origin of the Species, "To suppose that the eye with all its inimitable contrivances for adjusting the focus to different distances, for admitting different amounts of light, and for the correction of spherical and chromatic aberration, could have been formed by natural selection, seems, I freely confess, absurd in the highest degree." (Although he believed that the "absurd in the highest degree" happened.)

The likelihood of the complexity of the human eye evolving by random chance (plus time) is nothing compared to the likelihood of living cells with their incredibly complex DNA molecules, evolving by random chance (plus time).

But what concerned me about the theory of evolution was that it seemed to me that the logical conclusion is that there is no meaning or purpose to life.

Why would I think that? Because if there is no designer of human life, no designer of sunsets and rainbows, no designer of smiles and love and joy, and puppies and babies, mountains and cool breezes; and there is no purpose behind it all- if it is all just a bunch of freak accidents, then we are no better and are of no more value than a cockroach, a piece of manure or a rock. We just happened to turn out differently.

Love is a Survival Instinct?

My mother had a boyfriend who was a retired biology professor. We discussed the theory of evolution one day and he tried to assure me that it was true and that as he said, love is just a survival instinct that our species developed by chance, that helps the species to propagate. So, love is just a survival instinct like that of a maggot that moves a certain way to avoid injury? Hmm. No wonder so many people think life is meaningless.

It seemed to me that we could pretend that life has purpose, but that thought process would really just be (as my biology professor friend said) something that randomly evolved, that happens to result in our species continuing to survive. So, who are we to say that we should live and that flesh-eating bacteria that is attacking a sick person, should die?

If "survival of the fittest" is what determines what should survive and what shouldn't, then why not breed cockroaches? They seem very adaptable to things like "climate change." Who are we to think that we are more fit to survive? And who are we to say that something that is "more fit" should survive rather than something else?

Adolf Hitler, Joseph Stalin, Vladimir Lenin, Mao Tse-tung and Pol Pot were influenced by Darwin's theory of evolution and killed (around) 100 million people. (But of course, we can't say it was all Darwin's fault.)

Adolph Hitler was enthralled by Darwin's theory of evolution. He was working toward developing a "master race" and was working to kill off what he thought were "inferior races."

The full title of Charles Darwin's history changing book was, *On the Origin of Species by Means of Natural Selection, or the Preservation of Favoured Races in the Struggle for Life*. (Emphasis added.) Notice that he doesn't say "Favored *Species*," he says, "Favored *Races*." It's a very racist theory! Adolf Hitler was responsible for millions of people being killed- millions of those who he thought were inferior.

Charles Darwin wrote some very racist things, such as, "At some future period ... the civilized races of man will almost certainly exterminate, and replace, the savage races throughout the world."[1]

After reading Darwin's writing, Adolph Hitler wrote, "the highest aim of human existence is not the maintenance of a State or Government but rather the conservation of the race ... we cannot admit that one race is equal to another. ... races of superior and inferior quality... For in a world which would be composed of mongrels and [racial epithet for black people deleted] all ideals of human beauty and nobility and all hopes of an idealized future for our humanity would be lost forever."[2]

---

[1] Charles Darwin, The Descent of Man
[2] Adolph Hitler, Mein Kampf

If random chance evolutionary theory is true, isn't it logical to conclude that some races of people may be more evolved than others and may in fact be "superior"? The theory of evolution seems to me to be an extremely racist theory.

Hitler's methods of killing people were horribly inhumane, but wouldn't someone who really buys into the theory of evolution think that what Hitler was doing was possibly helpful to the human species?

If Darwinian random chance evolution is really how we all got to be human, how can anyone rightly say that it is "wrong" to cause pain and suffering? How can one series of freak accidents (you and me) say that another series of freak accidents (like Hitler, Stalin, Lenin, Mao Tse-tung and Pol Pot) are doing something "wrong"? How can anyone rightly say that there is such a thing as good and evil? Or right and wrong?

If the theory of evolution is true, then if a man and his five-year-old son are hiking on a mountain trail and a hungry mountain lion comes charging out of the brush toward the little boy, why should the man protect the boy? The lion needs to eat to survive.

More Important than a Maggot?

How can human beings rightly say that we are "better" or "more important" or more deserving to live, than a lion or a slug, a maggot or the bacteria that causes bubonic plague? How can we say that we are of any more value or importance than a rock? How can we even say that life is better than non-life? If evolution is just a bunch of coincidences that happen, like the wind blowing one way or another way around a hill, then it seems unreasonable for us to pretend that there is such a thing as meaning or purpose in life.

I started thinking about this and it caused me to lose hope. If we are just freak accidents, then there really is no purpose or reason for our existence. We just like to pretend there is. It's no wonder that so many people in my generation and now the millennial generation have no hope.

I had youth and good health. I loved surfing. It was kind of a god to me. The thrills I experienced while surfing on O'ahu's North Shore, were amazing and unlike any other thrills I had ever experienced (although flying in my dreams was also thrilling). I usually surfed at a spot called Pipeline, which was incredibly exhilarating. I "fell in love" in my senior year in high school. I also had three loving sisters and loved my parents. I had a lot going for me. I had youth, health, romance and thrills, but my life lacked a deep sense of peace. Life had no purpose or meaning.

Why are we alive? Just to work, have fun, try to be "good," maybe have children who will work, have fun, try to be "good," who might have children who will work, have fun, try to be "good"... and then we all just die? Why? Why are we here?

At the time, I thought, "Maybe if I just make a lot of money, all the pieces of my life will come together, and I'll have that deep sense of peace that I've been looking for."

That was before I had the most amazing supernatural experience of my life.

3

A Reed in the Wind

I started smoking pot toward the end of my senior year in high school. It was an effective diversion that kept me from thinking about the realities of what I considered to be, our meaningless existence. I went to college for a few years (in Hawai'i and California) but didn't work toward getting a college degree since I planned to start my own business and didn't think a degree would be of any use to me. I took classes that I thought would be useful (business, English, accounting...) as well as classes that I was interested in, like art, logic, astronomy, psychology and oceanography.

I also started cleaning high-rise windows because of a suggestion made by my mother. She figured that since I had surfed on the North Shore of O'ahu for years, I probably would be brave enough to hang from a high-rise building on a rope, and she had met a couple of window cleaners who told her they liked their jobs. My mother didn't know I had a fear of heights.

At the time my mother suggested window cleaning to me, I was on a quest to overcome fear, since it seemed to be a significant hindrance in my life. I figured that the way to overcome fear was to confront it head on, so when my mother mentioned high-rise window cleaning, I thought it would be a great way to overcome my fear of heights.

I attended college in Hawai'i for a year, then a year in San Diego, then back to Hawai'i and back again to California (Costa Mesa). I was enjoying life; going to college, cleaning windows, smoking pot and surfing. And I was having out-of-body experiences; more and more of them. I would fly over the clouds and fly from Canada to South America in a fraction of a second. I was soaring up above beautiful fields and between trees in New Zealand. Going to Africa. On and on it went. I had a life in the daytime and a life at night while my body was (supposedly) sleeping. It was amazing. I had no fear of death because I had become so accustomed to being out of my body, I thought death would be a very easy thing to go through.

While I was living in San Diego, I came across a book entitled, The Teachings of Don Juan, written by a man named Carlos Castaneda, a man who Time Magazine has called "the father of the new age." He was an anthropologist who reportedly studied under some shamans in Mexico. The book rocked my world. It had taken me years of practice to learn how to have out-of-body experiences where I could effectively move and fly. I had been slowly developing my abilities to have these experiences since I first started having them about 15 years earlier. Then I read Carlos Castaneda's book. It perfectly described the techniques that had taken me so many years to learn. He even used the same terminology. He talked about directing one's "will." He perfectly described the experiences I was having- the heightened state of awareness, etc. I was astounded. Then I read another book by Mr. Castaneda, then another and another until I had read all five of his books that he had written.

A Problem

I was devouring Castenada's books, but I got to a point in one of them that really troubled me. There was an apprentice who needed to walk off a cliff in order to show that he had fully mastered the techniques he had learned. Needless to say, it didn't strike me as being a good thing to (even indirectly) encourage people to walk off cliffs as they seek to master techniques along the road to spiritual enlightenment. I shudder when I think that some people (out of the millions of people who have read his books) may have actually followed the example in that book.

I lived in Costa Mesa, California for a year and attended Orange Coast Community College. By this time, I had been cleaning high-rise windows for a few years. I bought a 1967 Volkswagen van, which I equipped with a sink that I had found in a trash can while looking for things to put together for an art class assignment. (I was directed to make an art piece that had a "post nuclear" theme.) I also built a bed in the van along with some racks where I could safely hang my surfboards.

It was the perfect set-up. I cleaned windows part time, attended college part time, surfed and lived in my van. I could park my van on a bluff and sit and watch the sunset while I ate my dinner, go to sleep and wake up and go surfing and then head to class, or I could park next to a building where I was cleaning windows and wake up and go to work without driving in rush hour traffic. And I started making more money than I had ever made previously. Window cleaning pays well compared to the jobs I had previously, and since many cities around the world have job opportunities for window cleaners, I figured I could live where I wanted to live, travel, surf and live a happy life. But my life still lacked a deep sense of peace and meaning.

I took a Philosophy class at Orange Coast College. I was on a mission. Could any of these guys (philosophers through the ages) explain the meaning of life? Could they reveal that there actually is purpose in life? Could they help me to find that deep, abiding sense of peace?

Over thousands of years, men like Aristotle, Kant, Nietzsche, Sartre, Plato, Russell, Hume, Descartes, and others, have all sought to put the pieces together. Why are we here? (And even, "Are we here?") What is the meaning and purpose to life? As I read through insights, theories and perspectives of these men, I did it with a purpose. I wasn't just curious as to their perspectives; I was searching for truth.

In the case of most of them, I was able to discredit their explanations and conclusions (at least in my mind) because they did not acknowledge a very real part our existence that I knew existed- the spiritual realm. How can anyone give an adequate explanation of life and the world, when they are giving a three-dimensional description of a world that is comprised of more than just three-dimensions? To my dismay, as I studied the teachings of these great minds of history, I (in my mind at least) discredited one after another.

There was one man who (in my estimation) I couldn't discredit- a guy named Augustine, who I had never heard of before. He not only accounted for physical existence, but he acknowledged the spiritual realm as well. However, he believed there was a God; a God who created human beings for a purpose, and it was a purpose that I was not at all comfortable with. As Augustine said, "Oh, God, You have created us for Yourself, so that our hearts are restless until they find their rest in You." I had heard this idea expressed in another way- "We all have a God-shaped hole in our life, and we will never find true satisfaction unless we fill that hole with God."

Weak People Who Need Something to Believe In

I had been exposed to some Christians in my life and had concluded that they are weak people who need something to believe in. It seemed like it was a crutch for them. I figured that all religions had bits of truth and we can take what we want from each one (or none of them) and find what works for us. We can each have "our own truth."

It seemed to me that all religions had good ethical teachings and I was impressed by the morality of Buddhism.

There was only one religion I thought I knew was wrong. That religion was Biblical Christianity. I was vaguely familiar with the message. God loves people, but we are separated from "Him" by our sins (wrongs we have done), and the only way to be reconciled to God is through Jesus Christ. I thought, "You mean to tell me that all the Hindus, Muslims and Buddhists in the world are going to Hell because they don't have Jesus?! That is far too narrow!" There is no way I could accept such a ridiculous sounding scenario. I didn't know which, if any religion was a true religion, but Biblical Christianity was the one religion I "knew" was false.

So, when I read some of the philosophy of Augustine, I figured, ok, I can substitute the word "infinite" for his uses of the word "God" and I then couldn't discredit the things he taught. But I didn't dig deeper to find out more of what Augustine taught. After all, he was a Christian and I had no interest in that "nonsense."

"Anything But That!"

One day, I was sitting in my van, on the border between the towns of Santa Ana and Costa Mesa, thinking about life. I had dated a number of girls during the two years I lived in California. I had youth, health, thrills, romance, and now I was making more money than I ever had in my life. I could travel where I wanted to travel and live where I wanted to live, but I still didn't have that deep sense of peace. I thought to myself, "You live, work, party, life is a bummer at times, and then you die. Maybe you have kids. They live, work, party, life is a bummer at times, then they die. Maybe they have kids. They live, work, party, life is a bummer at times…" It's like mice running on one of those little running wheels. They run and run and don't get anywhere. I thought, "There has to be more to life!" As I sat in my van thinking this, for some reason, I unintentionally turned my head to my left. My glance came to rest on a cross that was on top of a steeple of a church. There were some trees between the church and me, so I couldn't see the church building. All I could see was the tip of the pointed steeple- and the cross. The cross was facing straight toward me and was perfectly framed by the trees. I hadn't glanced past the cross and then looked back after noticing it. I thought, "… There has to be more to life," and then I turned my head and looked straight at the cross.

My response was immediate and adamant, "Oh! Anything but that!" I was repulsed! I was searching, but if there was one thing I wasn't searching for, that was it! The last thing I wanted was to become a "Jesus freak."

A few days later, as I was sitting in my van, I again started thinking along the same lines, "There has to be more to life- you live, work, party, you try to be a good person, life is a bummer at times, and then you get old and die…" For some reason, I turned my head to my left. Again, I found myself looking straight at a cross that was on top of a church, perfectly framed between some trees. Again, I couldn't see the church building, just the cross, facing straight toward me. I had the same strong reaction I did the first time- "Oh! Anything but that!"

One afternoon, a few days later, I was sitting in a park. I started thinking the same things about life. Yup, you guessed it. The same thing happened again. I turned my head and looked straight at a cross, perfectly framed between two trees. The same thing happened again, and again and again and again- seven times in two weeks!

Immediately after thinking, "There has to be more to life..." I looked straight at a cross on top of a church. Not once did I see the edge of a cross. Not once was it at an angle. Every time, it was facing straight toward me, perfectly framed and centered between the trees. And not once did I see a church building- just the cross. This happened over and over again, while I was sitting in different places all around the Costa Mesa and Santa Anna area.

I felt very strongly about seeing those crosses. I thought, "Christianity is a crutch for weak people who need something to believe in. Let them have their thing but I don't want to hear about it!"

Power Beyond Anything I Had Ever Known

One day, around the same time as I was having these "cross" experiences, I took a walk in a wilderness area near Newport beach. As I walked along, I suddenly became aware of a tremendous power right next to me. It's difficult to describe the sensation. All I can say is that it was like nothing I'd ever experienced. I turned to my right and it seemed that in this clearing I was now facing, there was a power far greater than anything I had ever known.

Usually, in my spiritual quests, I was seeking spiritual enlightenment, power or ability. But the power in front of me was so awesome, that for the first time in my life, I felt like I needed to humble myself in front of it. But at the same time, I wanted proof that this power was real. I spoke out loud, "Please forgive me, but if there is power here, please give me a sign." A reed that was about three feet long, suddenly popped up in front of me. It stood straight up. Wow! That was amazing! But it wasn't enough. I wanted to know with absolute certainty that this spiritual force was real.

After all, I reasoned, what if when I asked that question, the tip of that reed had been under another reed that was under one of my feet and when I asked the question, maybe I leaned back ever so slightly and like a spring-loaded trigger, it was released and popped up? (This didn't seem like a likely explanation at all, but I figured it could somehow be a remote possibility.) I thought, "I need to know that I know that this is real."

I humbled myself again, even more this time. "Please forgive me, but if there is power here, please give me one more sign." The same reed that was standing straight up in front of me, let out a snap like a yard stick that is snapped in half- "Crack!" I then saw and heard it rattle back to a standstill (standing straight up). The moment the reed snapped; I was flooded from head to toe with a message. Within a three-year period of my turning 40 years old (I was 20 at the time), I was going to be connected to a multitude of people. And the spiritual force that connected us was going to "move mountains."

I had no idea what this meant, but it was an incredible experience. The power was tremendous, and to me, it was an undeniable confirmation that there was indeed a very real spiritual power beyond anything I had ever known.

Running on Empty

There were several other miraculous sorts of things that happened to me around the same time. One was when my friend Stephen and I decided we would make a surf trip into Baja Mexico. We decided to take my van that I had modified to make more Baja friendly. It was a memorable trip to say the least (ending up in a Mexican jail for driving drunk, running people off the road and then crashing into a ditch, etc.) but one of (a few) amazing things that happened on that trip was when we ran out of gas.

I had run out of gas previously in this van and found out the hard way that the gas gauge was very accurate. The van would run out of gas right when the gas gauge needle was on the empty mark. But not this time. When I noticed that the gas gauge showed that the van was out of gas, I looked at the odometer to see how many miles we had driven.

Somehow, the van kept on going. We were quite a distance from a gas station, but the van just kept right on driving. We drove 5, 10, 15, 20 miles- the van kept on going. The engine finally died as we were driving down a hill- about 70 feet from the gas station. We coasted up to the gas pump after driving 40 miles on empty!

Due to some major mechanical problems on the van, we had to take the engine out of the van on this trip. The muffler also fell off the van about 10 miles away from Costa Mesa (where we lived). When we drove into my friend's driveway back in Costa Mesa, the engine died, and we coasted to a stop in the driveway parking spot.

It almost seemed like someone (or something) was watching out for us.

By this point, you might be thinking I was having marijuana induced hallucinations or that I was just delusional. And that may seem like a logical explanation, but evidence started stacking up to prove that I was not imagining things.

4

Proof I Wasn't Crazy

I moved back to Hawai'i after that year of college and enrolled in the University of Hawai'i. I was surfing a lot. I rented a house with six other guys. (What a mess!) For a while, my friend Dino and I kept track on a calendar. At one point, we had surfed 45 times in 30 days. We were surfing a lot at night as well (if there was enough moonlight to surf by). I was also cleaning windows, having spiritual experiences, and taking some college classes, although my academic achievements were nothing at all to brag about. I dropped out of some classes and did ok in others.

I was smoking pot pretty much every day. On most days I smoked in the morning when I woke up, at lunch time, after work or school, and then again in the evening. Life didn't have any purpose or meaning- why not get stoned? I usually drank a beer after work and sometimes on weekends I would drink a six-pack or two.

The number and type of my spiritual experiences was increasing. I started buying crystals from a shop that shared space with the local health food store. I could hold different types of crystals in my hand and sense their properties. For example, I would hold a type of crystal and think, "This feels like it would be good for healing..." I would then look in a book on crystals and see that sure enough, that type of crystal is supposed to be good for healing. It was very confirming for me. I was "tuned in" to the spiritual realm.

Here Kitty, Kitty!

One night a few years later (I was living with my window cleaning business partner, Will, and his psychic wife), I closed my bedroom door and as I lay down on my bed to go to sleep, I drifted part way to sleep. I felt the mattress next to my body being pressed downward by the weight of something walking on the mattress alongside my body, a few inches away from me. We didn't have any pets, so it was a big surprise. I reached my arm out to my side to touch it but there was nothing there. I turned on the bedroom light and looked around the room. There was no animal in the room and the door was closed. That was weird. I lay back down, and a few minutes later, again felt the weight of what seemed to be a cat (I could hear it purring), pushing down on the mattress, walking next to me. It started next to my knee and walked up toward the head of the bed. This time I reached my arm out quickly. If there was a cat there, I was going to make contact with it. My hand swooped through the air without making contact with anything. Hmm. Nothing there.

I again turned on the light and thoroughly searched the room- no cat. I turned off the light and lay back down on the bed. A few minutes later the same thing happened again. I whipped my arm across where I felt the cat to be but there was nothing there. Light on, search made- no cat. I laid back down again, getting quite freaked out by this bizarre occurrence. It happened again. This time I didn't reach my arm out right away because I wanted to see what would happen, and it felt like the cat walked alongside of my body and then started to step over across my neck. I could feel the hair on the back of my neck go up as the cat's hairs seemed to barely touch them. I reached my hand up quickly and hit the back of my neck. There was no cat stepping over me.

Lights on, search made. Again- no cat! Am I losing my marbles? (Wait, don't answer that question!) The next morning, I woke up and got in my car to drive to work. In the middle of the driveway was a kitten that had been hit and killed by a car the night before. I got out of my car and disposed of the cat's body. It was definitely not a hallucination.

UFO's Anyone?

My psychic roommate made the psychics I saw on TV look like amateurs. She would sometimes relay perfectly accurate information she received from the spirits she "channeled." On one occasion, I asked her a question about a possible move of an organization that she knew nothing about. She connected to her spirits and said that yes, the organization was going to move to a place with a bunch of small wooden buildings- like cabins.

It was something she couldn't possibly have known anything about. I found out later that indeed, the organization was in negotiations about possibly moving to a location with a bunch of small wooden buildings- like cabins. While the information about the possible new location was perfectly accurate, the organization didn't end up moving at all.

On other occasions, she (and the spirits she was channeling) would be completely wrong. I noticed that the spirits she was "channeling" seemed to be able to describe current events but were apparently only able to guess at the future.

One night as the psychic and I walked along Diamond Head beach (I don't remember if Will was there), we decided that we would try to contact a UFO. The psychic and I looked up into the night sky and she said, "If you are up there, give us a 'Hi.'" Immediately, out from behind a cloud came two small lights. (They looked like very bright stars.) They were next to each other and moved parallel to each other in a straight line quickly across part of the sky (at a speed that looked about the same as the speed a meteorite travels across the sky). But then they both suddenly made a sharp, 90-degree angle change of direction and moved (still next to each other) in a straight line and disappeared behind another cloud.

The psychic and I discussed what we had just seen. We both saw the exact same phenomenon- two lights came out from behind a cloud, made a sharp, 90-degree change of direction at the same instant and then disappeared behind another cloud. How can you explain something like this? We both had the same hallucination at the same time? Are there aliens that we can communicate with through our thoughts? If you are a skeptic like me, I know what you are probably thinking, "Yeah, right! Sure! What a bunch of bologna!" But hold on.

I am not saying those lights belonged to UFO's. I'm not saying that we communicated with extra-terrestrial beings. I'm just telling you our experiences. Right after the psychic spoke toward the sky, we both saw two lights travel across the sky in a way that aircraft and meteorites, etc. cannot possibly travel.

Proof that Out-of-body Experiences are Real?

There was a radio station in Honolulu that I used to listen to that had a talk show featuring a woman named Alice Ann Parker. She would interpret people's dreams and I could tell by her interpretations; she wasn't just looking for symbolism in the dreams. She was also using her psychic abilities to interpret the dreams.

I called the talk show one Friday night and asked Alice Ann what she thought about out-of-body experiences. She said, "Oh, they're real. Do you have them?" I said yes. She said, "Take me flying!"

A few nights later, I contacted her in my sleep by calling her name. I felt myself instantly travel across the island. I was outside of a custom-built house on the north side of the island. I could see (through the walls) that a woman (wearing red) was standing in the kitchen. Another slightly larger woman stood next to her. The house was elevated off the ground by about a foot and a half and had faded grey stain on the walls. "I" went in through the wall and got more of a look at the inside of the house. It had a small square kitchen and a small square living room on the left (with a closet with sliding wooden doors). There was a hallway that ran along the right side of the kitchen and I saw two dog dishes next to the door on the far side of the kitchen. (The door led out onto a concrete patio.)

I left and then when the next Friday evening came around, I called the talk show again. "You came and visited me the other night," Alice Ann said. "That's right," I replied. "You came into my kitchen," she said. "That's right," I replied again. "Describe to me what it looked like," she said.

I described the house and kitchen (although I didn't ask her whether there was another woman in the house with her). She told me it sounded exactly right (and that she had been wearing red) and asked me to send her a drawing of the layout of her house. I drew the layout of the house and sent it to her in the mail.

On the next Friday's program, I called her again, and she told me that I had drawn a perfectly accurate diagram of her house; except for two things. First, the dog dishes that I drew next to the kitchen door, were next to that door, but they were outside of that wall, not inside of the wall (where I had placed them in the drawing). That was an easy mistake for me to make, since I could "see" through the walls and the dog dishes were in line with where I drew them, they were just outside of that wall, not inside of it.

The second discrepancy could not be explained away so easily. She said that the entire drawing was exactly flipped. It was like a mirror image. So, the hallway I saw to the right of the kitchen, was actually on the left side of the kitchen. And the small, square living room that I saw to the left of the kitchen was actually on the right side of the kitchen. There was something very wrong about this experience. It was a big red flag for me, but at the time, I didn't know what to make of it.

A couple of months later I was thumbing through a magazine and I opened it to a page and looked at a photograph. I immediately recognized the person in the photo. There was no mistaking it. It was Alice Ann Parker. I looked at the caption under the photograph. It confirmed that it was indeed a photo of her. That was another confirmation for me of the validity of my out-of-body experiences. But the discrepancies regarding my almost perfect drawing were not nearly as "confirming."

The discrepancy with the dog dishes was a small mistake to have made, but if you walk into someone's house, and then describe it a few days later, you wouldn't make the mistake of thinking that everything that was on the left side of the house, was actually on the right side. You were there! You saw it! How can you make a mistake like that? I don't think you can. Something was very wrong. It was a custom-built home and I experienced and described it accurately- but it was all backwards- a mirror image. I didn't know what to make of it, but something was definitely wrong with the picture.

And my eyes were about to be opened in a way they never had been before.

5

Planets and an Offering

I was very involved in the "New Age" movement and had a number of different of kinds of experiences. I can't give you any proof that this particular event happened, but I will share it since it seemed significant to me at the time. One day I decided to try to dissolve a cloud in the sky using my mental abilities. There were a bunch of clouds in one particular area of the sky. I focused on the one in the middle and attempted to make it dissolve. Within a couple of seconds, it disappeared, and I watched as the other clouds drifted across the sky with a patch of blue sky in the middle. I had quite a few other experiences (including meditation and an out-of-body encounter with "evil" extra-terrestrials in Siberia) that I won't go into detail about here, but I will share a couple of other experiences I had. One that seemed to confirm spiritual realities and another one that caused me to question some of my underlying beliefs about reality.

In 1987, I heard about an event that was going to happen in August of that year. I was 27 years old, and the number of spiritual experiences I was having, was increasing and becoming more varied.

A man named Jose Arguelles (along with some others) wrote about an event (that reportedly tied in with the Mayan calendar and Aztec prophecies) in which the planets in our solar system were supposedly aligning in a way that would be part of a "harmonic convergence" in which the "energy" of earth would shift from being "warlike" to being "peaceful." (Looking back now, it doesn't seem like that shift happened.)

Mr. Arguelles had written about some events that were supposed to help usher in this phenomenon. He said that 144,000 people all around the world, would gather in small groups and help to bring about this planetary change. I had a printout of (several pages of) what he said would happen. I hadn't read through it but had heard a little about what was supposed to happen.

To my surprise, I myself was one of those people who performed certain rituals that he said would need to be performed during that period of several days in August. I "danced" around a fire (a candle I had lit) in clockwise circles (this was prior to me reading that this was precisely what people would do), and I (along with several friends who were camping with me) saw numerous flashes of light (at the same time) on the periphery of our vision (as I would say, "out of the corner of my eye"). Several of these bright flashes came from the Pali (the cliff) that was about 1,000 feet tall (that had no sources of light). A few of us also saw flashes of light on the periphery of our vision as we sat on Kailua beach watching the sun rise the next morning.

One of the things that amazed me the most about the events of these few days, was that I hadn't read about exactly what was supposed to happen. But I was doing things and we were experiencing things that were predicted in the writings; things that I hadn't even read about yet.

I didn't know why I felt compelled to light a candle and dance (my "dance" was actually more of a walk than a dance) around it in a clockwise circle. I just felt like I should do it. And I didn't know about the flashes of light, but five or six of us all saw them- at the same exact times. Having those experiences and then reading afterward, that those were the experiences that people were predicted to have, confirmed to me that I was having valid spiritual experiences involving real spiritual forces.

Different Kinds of Spirits

Up to this point, I hadn't really encountered "evil" spirits (other than the "evil" alien beings I believed I had encountered in an out-of-body experience in Siberia). I assumed (without really thinking it through) that spiritual forces were good, could be trusted and were reliable sources of information. I had kind of a "If it's spiritual, it must be good and true," kind of mindset.

Several encounters I had were with Hawai'ian spiritual forces. Since I was born and raised in Hawai'i and was interested in all things spiritual, I developed an interest in Hawai'ian spirituality. I started reading about the subject. One day, I thought I would present an offering to the Hawai'ian gods. I drove my car up the Pali Highway and pulled over near the point of the highway with the highest elevation (near the Pali lookout). I took an offering of fruit that I had prepared and wrapped in tea leaves, got out of my car and walked into the forest and placed my offering in the crook of a tree. I felt good about making an offering to the gods.

As I got back into my car, it occurred to me; I had forgotten to put Hawai'ian rock salt in with the offering. (I had read that that was the proper way to make the offering.) I wanted to do things right, so I drove to my apartment, got some Hawai'ian rock salt and drove back up to the Pali to put the salt on the offering. I got out of my car with the salt and started to walk back toward where I had placed the offering. I got about 60 feet away from the tree where I had placed it and suddenly walked into what felt like a solid wall of evil. I stopped dead in my tracks. It was by a million times, the darkest, heaviest, most evil presence I had ever experienced in my life. I had never experienced or even imagined anything like it. I had no idea that such an extremely evil force existed. I didn't dare walk any closer to the offering. I hurried back to my car and drove home.

I was in shock. Here I was, making an offering to the gods. As far as I was concerned, I had nothing but good intentions, and I thought that surely the gods would be pleased with my offering. The thought came to mind, "Are these the gods that I have been trying to please? Is this what they are really like?" I was astounded.

Not too long after this experience, I made a phone call to one of the (numerous) leaders of the Hawai'ian spiritual/political movement which was having somewhat of a resurgence at the time. He had written a book on Hawai'ian spirituality and seemed quite knowledgeable on the subject.

I asked him about a couple of aspects of the Hawai'ian religion that troubled me; aspects that you don't hear discussed much in public. He was telling me how good the Hawai'ian religion is and how it should be revived. I said, "But what about human sacrifice and cannibalism? That's was part of the Hawai'ian religion as well." His response surprised me. He said, "The only reason people don't participate in cannibalism now is because they don't know how good people taste." He then went on to tell me that he had made a trip to Samoa and indicated that he had participated in cannibalism.

I should probably point out that many of the Hawai'ian people I have known in my life are among the most loving, kind people I have ever met. There is a tremendous beauty to their spirit of Aloha, and they are extremely giving and generous. I also should point out that a religion that includes human sacrifice and cannibalism is not the only religion that has been a big part of Hawai'ian history.

Many people (even many Hawai'ians) don't know that at one point in the early 1800's, Hewa, the high priest of Hawai'i, completely independent of any foreign missionaries' influence, declared that the religion being practiced in Hawai'i was a false religion. (For example, one of many false beliefs was that if men and women ate a meal together, they would die.) Hewa ordered all the Heiaus (places of worship where people would make sacrifices) in Hawai'i to be demolished. He said he had a vision of a God of light that would be coming to Hawai'i.

Within a few months, the first missionaries arrived in Hawai'i and so many Hawai'ian people turned to the God of the Bible, that at one point, more than 90% of the population of Hawai'i had reportedly become Christians. Haili Church in Hilo became the largest church in the world, with a congregation of over 10,000 members. There has never been a nation (prior to or since that time) that has had such a high percentage of Christians as Hawai'i did at that point. So, the religion that included human sacrifice and cannibalism is definitely not the only spirituality the Hawai'ian people have known.

A New Direction

One day, I was thinking about all of the spiritual experiences I had had in my life, I thought to myself, "Where am I going in my spiritual life?" Unintentionally, I turned my head and looked directly at a cross that was on top of a church. The cross was facing directly toward me and I couldn't see the church that the cross was on top of because it was blocked by some trees. I just saw the cross- perfectly framed by the trees. Wow. It had been about 10 years since I had those experiences of looking directly at those crosses, and it was definitely a surprise to have it happen again.

A few days later, it happened again, then again, and again. Over and over, during the next week and a half or so, I found myself staring straight at crosses, after wondering about where I was heading in my spiritual life. One of those times, I was standing in front of the kitchen sink in my apartment. As I was thinking about my spiritual life, I looked out the window (straight in front of me) and I noticed for the first time, that the view from my apartment window (above the neighbor's rooftop) consisted of two things- the tip of Diamond Head, and a cross, facing directly toward me (it was on top of the chapel of Sacred Hearts Academy). Wow. I hadn't noticed that before.

A few days later, I was in my "bosun chair" (like a swing) hanging on a rope on the 21st floor of a building in downtown Honolulu. As I cleaned a window, I started thinking about what the sources of all of my spiritual experiences could be. It seemed to me that I couldn't know for certain what the sources of many of my experiences were.

Was it really a Hawai'ian spirit that spoke to me? Was it really the spirit of a cat that had died that was "walking" on my bed? Did I really see the lights of a UFO? Was I absolutely certain that my spirit or soul was really traveling outside of my body?

I had strong evidence to confirm that those experiences were spiritual in nature, but what were the spiritual entities I was interacting with? I couldn't say with absolute certainty.

Then I thought, "But what about seeing those crosses, so perfectly positioned, at such precise moments in time? Those had to be signs from God. Who or what else would want me to look at those crosses?" I turned my head to my right. This time, for the first time, I did it intentionally. I wanted to see if I would look at a cross. Honolulu (like every other city) is full of lines; mostly vertical and horizontal- lots of buildings. At the pinpoint I looked at (about ¾ mile away) I didn't see a cross. "Still," I thought, "those had to be signs from God." Unintentionally, I turned my head again and looked back at the exact spot I had looked at the moment before, and there actually was a cross there! I just hadn't seen it the first time I looked! This time however, the church was facing to the right. Because the church was so far away and was facing to my right, the cross looked like a tiny straight line (like looking at a needle from about 5 feet away). And this time, I could see the whole front of the church building, not just the cross and the tip of the steeple. But it was a cross, at the exact pinpoint I had looked at the moment earlier. I was amazed.

A few days later, I was cleaning the windows on another building in Honolulu (Nu'uanu) and as I walked along on the building rooftop, I was now really wondering about it. I wondered aloud, "So who is it that is calling me like this? Who is it that is showing me all those crosses, so perfectly positioned, at such precise moments? Is it 'God,' whatever 'God' is? (There are so many different and contradictory versions of who or what 'God' is.) Or is it Jesus and the God of the Bible?" As I was asking this question, I walked around the corner of a wall that extended up above the building rooftop. As I came around the corner, there were two walls (about 8 feet tall) that were extending about 25 feet in front of me. A third wall (that was about chest high) extended between the ends of the two walls.

As I walked around the corner, directly in front of me was a giant white cross, perfectly centered and framed between the two walls (right above the shorter wall). Because of perspective, it looked like everything was  pointing to this giant cross. As I came around the corner, the split second the word "Jesus" was starting to come out of my mouth, I was staring directly at a giant white cross. Wow! "Who is calling me like this? Is it 'God,' whatever 'God' is, or is it Jesus and the God of the Bible?" It was instantly clear. It was Jesus and the God of the Bible.

Like I said, I am a skeptic and am quite stubborn (and had no interest whatsoever in Christianity). I didn't fall down on my knees and pray or anything, but I thought, "I guess I better check this thing out."

6

Who Wrote This Book?

The next building I was working on was directly across the street from an old theater that had been turned into a church- Calvary Chapel Honolulu. On my lunch break, I walked across the street and into the church. There was a gal sitting at the front desk. "Do you sell Bibles here?" I asked. "Sure, what kind would you like?" I thought that was a strange question. I said something like, "Oh, medium; blue, black- whatever." She explained to me that there were a number of good translations that differed slightly but that they all said the same things.

I asked, "What do you think about out-of-body experiences?" She said, "Well, the Bible says that demons are real spiritual beings and that they can deceive people." I just grunted, "Hmm." I then asked, "What do you think about spirits speaking to people in foreign languages?" Again, she replied by telling me what the Bible says about spirits that seek to deceive people. In response to every question I asked about what she believed, rather than telling me what she believed, she directed me to what the Bible says. I found out later, that Valerie was not just a church secretary. She was also very knowledgeable about the Bible.

She told me about KLHT, the Calvary Chapel radio station and I took my new (maroon colored) Bible and went home. I started reading the Bible (in the New Testament, the second part of the Bible) and started listening to the Christian radio station when I had time.

As I was reading along, one verse seemed to almost jump off the page at me. In the book of John, Jesus said, "You did not choose Me, but I chose you..."¹ I thought, "That's for sure, because I sure didn't choose YOU!" As far as I was concerned, Jesus was about the last thing I would choose.

I continued reading and another verse seemed to jump off the page at me. Jesus said, "What did you go out into the wilderness to see? A reed shaken by the wind?"² I looked in the footnote for that verse and saw that in the Greek (the language that the New Testament was originally written in), the word "wind" could also be translated as "spirit." So, another translation of that verse could be, "What did you go into the wilderness to see? A reed shaken by the spirit?"

I thought, "Who wrote this book?! This is not an ordinary book!" After going into the wilderness in California 10 years earlier and seeing a reed shaken by the most powerful spiritual force I had ever encountered, and then reading this verse; it got my attention. I had gone into the wilderness and seen "a reed shaken by the spirit." Obviously, that Bible verse was not just written with me in mind, but the fact that it precisely described the most powerful spiritual experience of my life, got my attention.

Starting to Listen

A few days later as I was sitting in my bedroom listening to the radio, it suddenly occurred to me that I was feeling the love of God coming through those guys on the radio. It was a strange realization because even though I was listening to a particular radio program, it all of a sudden felt like the love of God had been coming through the speakers of all of the programs I had been

---

¹ John 15:16
² Matthew 11:7

listening to. The main message being communicated by them was that God loves people, but we are separated from God because of our sins (missing the mark of true goodness), and that Jesus, who is God,[3] came down to this earth, took on human flesh, suffered and died to pay the penalty for our sins, and then rose from the dead on the third day. And that we can have our sins forgiven, be reconciled to God, and receive the free gift of eternal life (which will include eternity in Heaven). All we need to do is to repent from (change our mind about) our sins, turn to God and put our trust in Jesus as our Lord and Savior.

I had absolutely no interest in becoming a Christian, but what was I to do with all of this? How could I deny that God had shown me those crosses- over and over at those precise moments, when I was questioning life? How could I deny that God had been speaking to me through the Bible? How could I deny the amazing love of God that I felt coming through the radio? Experimentally, but whole-heartedly, as I sat on the floor in my bedroom, I prayed and said, "Ok, Jesus, if you are real, come into my life and forgive my sins."

The moment I prayed that prayer, I felt a peace that I had never known. It existed. It was real! And all of a sudden, it was mine! It wasn't a result of getting hyped up. It wasn't a result of meditating. It wasn't a "church thing." It was an experiment- a whole-hearted one, but an experiment- "Ok, Jesus, if you are real, come into my life and forgive my sins."

Many people don't experience any unusual feelings when receiving Jesus, but for me, all of a sudden, I had an indescribable peace. And I also couldn't get enough of reading the Bible. It was a sudden, insatiable appetite

---

[3] The Bible teaches that God is triune- God the Father, the Son (Jesus), and the Holy Spirit

for "God's Word." I read and read. It was as if I had an unquenchable thirst for the first 30 years of my life, that was suddenly realized and suddenly being quenched. It was amazing. As I read the Bible (and talked to God), it was like God was speaking directly to me over and over through the Bible- answering questions, giving me peace, truth, direction, emotional healing, and joy. I realized that we are not cosmic accidents. Our lives have tremendous meaning, purpose and significance. Each one of us was created by a loving, all-knowing, all-powerful God; a God who wants us to know Him.

A few days later, I told my mother about my having received Jesus into my life. That didn't go very well. I said, "I've become a Christian." She replied, "Not one of those 'born again' ones, I hope!" (She had been told that all "born again Christians" were former drug addicts who had traded their addiction to drugs, for an addiction to Jesus.) I replied in a mealy-mouthed way, "Well, some people might say..." She interrupted me, "You either are, or you aren't!" I couldn't deny that my life had been radically changed in a moment. "In that case," I replied, "I am." Her answer was expected. "Oh, great!" she said sarcastically.

Over the next few weeks, it became very clear to me that God didn't just want to be in my life, He wanted to "be my God." I needed to surrender to Him. I refer to God as "He" and "Him" because that's how the Bible refers to God. (I'll explain more in chapter 11 of this book.) Anyone can say they believe in God. The Bible says that even the demons believe there is a God.[4] I needed to acknowledge Him as God in my life. I needed to acknowledge Jesus as my "Lord" (allow Him to be in charge of my life). It was an easy step to make once I

---

4 James 2:19

realized how much He loves me. I prayed and asked Jesus to be my Lord.

My interests changed immediately after receiving Jesus. I stopped drinking all that beer. I threw thousands of dollars worth of crystals into the ocean. I broke all of my hard rock record albums (hundreds of them) in half and threw them in a dumpster. (For some reason, I no longer felt comfortable singing, "I'm on the highway to hell!")

I started going to church every time the doors were open. And on the evenings when they weren't open, I'd try to find another church that was open. And the church I was going to was nothing like the boring, dead religious church I attended as a child. It was filled with people who were filled with love and joy. During the "worship time" of music, I could feel the presence of God. And through the (verse-by-verse Bible teaching) sermons, God would speak to me and tell me things about my life-things I had been wondering about or concerned about, etc. The Bible teaching at the church was amazingly relevant to my life. If my friends from high school could see me now! I had become what I had loathed- a "Jesus freak!"

But I continued smoking pot. By this time, I had been smoking marijuana for more than 10 years. On most days, I smoked a little in the morning, a little at lunch time, a little after work and a little in the evening.

Turning Over an Old Leaf

About two months after becoming a follower of Jesus, I started to think that maybe God didn't want me to smoke pot. I had quit for a day or two, on four separate occasions during the previous 10 years. This time, I prayed and told God, "If you want me to quit, you are going to have to help me." He immediately took away the desire and I haven't smoked pot since that moment. It's now been about 30 years and even though I live in Washington state, where it is legal to smoke pot, I have no desire to smoke it- I have peace. I have purpose and meaning in life. I have a personal relationship with the Creator of the universe. Why in the world would I need to smoke pot?

I prayed to God about my out-of-body experiences. I had reached a point in my experiences in which I believed I could heal people while out of my body (although I hadn't yet done it). And out-of-body experiences were thrilling. But I knew I needed to surrender them to God.

I prayed to God, "If out-of-body experiences are of You, please increase them. But if they aren't, please protect me from them." They stopped immediately. I have had a few of them since then, but they have been few and far between and seem to always happen during times of what I would call, spiritual warfare. I believe the reason that what I saw at Alice Ann's house was a mirror image of the actual house, was because the entire experience was a deception- a vision planted in my mind by spiritual forces (demons) that are not aligned with God. The devil is real and is a master deceiver and a counterfeiter (and so are his demonic associates).

There are examples in the Bible of what some would call "out-of-body experiences," like when Paul the Apostle described an event in which a man, "whether in the body I do not know, or whether out of the body I do not know, God knows—such a one was caught up to the third heaven."[5] Such events seem to indicate that God may take people out of their bodies at times, but I am absolutely convinced that what millions of people think of as "out-of-body experiences" are not of God. They seem very real but are actually counterfeit experiences

---

[5] 2 Corinthians 12:2

implanted in people's minds by spiritual forces who aim to lead people away from a relationship with the true and living God.

Two of the reasons I am convinced of this are, first, the mirror image aspect of the house I "visited." There is no other explanation for the image of the house being reversed in my mind other than the explanation that I was not actually out of my body. I believe it was a vision being implanted in my mind. And secondly, even though the out-of-body experiences were thrilling, and I wanted to have more of them, they stopped immediately when I prayed about them.

Red Flags and Love

In thinking back about many of the spiritual experiences I had before asking Jesus into my life, I realize there were several other "red flags" over the years as well. I had brushed aside these "inconvenient truths" because they didn't fit in with my world view.

I had over a thousand out-of-body experiences over a period of 25 years (starting at age four) and I was astounded by the fact that they were interactions with spiritual forces who were intentionally deceiving me. They couldn't have simply been dreams, as my interactions with Alice Ann demonstrated. They were actual spiritual experiences. I was interacting with something, but I no longer believe that my spirit or soul was out of my body.

I believe I was interacting with a deceptive spiritual being (or beings) and when I intended to move or travel one way or another, the scenery would change, somewhat similar to a video game except that I also felt the sensation of movement (and flight). And whatever spiritual force (or forces) that I was interacting with was obviously intentionally deceiving me. Just because something is spiritual, does not mean it is good- or trustworthy.

When I think back about other experiences I had, I can see problems with them as well. I was quite excited as I presented my offering to the Hawai'ian "gods" but when I realized how absolutely evil they were, it shocked me. It didn't fit in with my formerly held beliefs that if something was spiritual, it must be good.

Talking with that expert in the Hawai'ian spiritual movement was also troubling. There is so much beauty and love expressed by so many of the people of Hawai'i. To hear that human (and animal) sacrifice and cannibalism are part of the (pre-Christian) Hawai'ian religion, was troubling to say the least.

Needless to say, reading the book by Carlos Castenada, (a very prominent New Age leader) that seemed to be encouraging walking off of cliffs to prove one's spirituality, was another red flag.

A counterfeit 100-dollar bill has many features that appear genuine. It is designed to look just like a real 100-dollar bill. But it doesn't matter how many people believe a counterfeit 100-dollar bill is real- it isn't. People may have been using counterfeit 100-dollar bills for their entire life and believe that they are 100% real. They may have worked well for people but that doesn't make them real.

One of my experiences with the "aliens" also raised a "red flag" in my mind (although it didn't at the time I experienced it). When I think back to that night on Diamond Head beach, there are things that don't seem to make sense. I was walking along the beach with a psychic (someone who, like me, was steeped in New Age spiritism) and we decided to try to make contact with aliens. Immediately after my psychic friend spoke out loud, saying something along the lines of, "If you are up there, give us a 'Hi,'" we both saw two lights that were next to each other, come out from behind a cloud, move in a straight line, make a sharp, 90 degree change in direction, move in a straight line and then disappear behind another cloud.

For those lights to be the distance they were from each other and to be at least as high as the clouds, if they belonged to the same UFO, that UFO would have to have been massive. Secondly, it's hard to imagine that aliens in a UFO would be able to hear (or sense) someone speak (the English language) on a beach, miles away, in the midst of so many other noises of the nearby city. Or might they have just read our minds? That seems hard to believe as well. Were they also reading the minds of the other 1 million people on the island of O'ahu? It's hard to believe that these aliens would somehow "hear" us, and then instantly turn on their lights to show that they are there, come out from behind a cloud and then disappear behind another cloud and/or turn off their lights.

The whole experience is hard to believe and if I hadn't lived through it, I probably wouldn't believe that it happened. But there is an explanation that makes sense. If there really are evil spiritual forces (demons), then it makes sense that they could easily orchestrate a little light show to convince people that there are indeed aliens from other planets who visit the earth. An interesting side note to the alien encounter is that it is common for people who say they have had alien encounters (sightings and abductions, etc.) to be involved in the occult (supernatural, mystical, or magical beliefs, practices, or phenomena).

What Valerie had told me when I walked into that church in Honolulu (about what the Bible teaches concerning spiritual forces that deceive people) started to really ring true when I looked back at my 25 years of spiritual experiences.

The spiritual experiences that I have had as a follower of Jesus have been very different than those I'd had earlier. Before I entered into a personal relationship with Jesus, my spiritual experiences almost always centered around my gaining spiritual power, ability, enlightenment, or experiencing a thrill of some kind.

As a Christian, I experienced something that I hadn't experienced in my previous spiritual experiences (although we talked about love a fair amount)- the absolutely amazing love of God. I have been a follower of Jesus for almost 30 years now and if there is one thing that I have learned more than anything else about God; it's that He loves us. We can be so self-centered, greedy and proud, and yet the God who is love, the God who is absolutely pure and perfect and who cannot lie or sin,[6] loves us. I fall so far short of perfection every day. I struggle with pride and selfishness and yet the God who hates pride and selfishness, loves me.

The God Who Loves Sinners

I think this might help to communicate my point.[7] I had been a Christian for about a year and a half. I was going to church on Sundays and was also going to church on Wednesday nights. I would tell people about God when it seemed like a good opportunity to talk about Him. I even carried around Gospel tracts in my pocket, (brochures) that had reasons why people should receive Jesus as their Lord and Savior. I was a "good" Christian.

I started to think God loved me because I was on His side. I was going to church and doing good deeds. I thought, "Of course, He should love me." One day I was tempted to commit a particular sin. It was something I knew the Bible says is wrong. As I thought about

---

[6] To lie or sin in any way would be against the nature of God. He is perfect and absolutely good.

[7] I also share this story in my other book, *The Place of Joy*

committing this sin, I thought, "This is wrong. I shouldn't do it, and I know the Bible says it's sin." I went ahead and did it anyway. Afterwards, I felt guilty. I had absolutely no excuse in the world for committing that sin. It was rebellion against God.

I prayed to God, "Lord, I knew that was a sin. I knew it before I did it and I did it anyway. There is no reason why You should forgive me, but I am asking You to forgive me." I am not one of those people who have lots of miraculous, supernatural experiences with God, but as those words finished coming out of my mouth, God touched me. It was as if His giant finger reached down out of Heaven and touched the top of my head. I was flooded from head to toe with an overwhelming sense of God's love.

It was as if God said to me a million times in a split second, "I love you. I love you. I love you." I was amazed. I couldn't believe it. I thought, "Who are You, God? How can You love me so much?" Here I was, immediately after committing a sin against God, and He was there telling me He loves me. It was as if He said to me, "You don't understand, Strat. I don't love you because of how wonderful you are or because you are trying to be good. I love you because of who I am."

The love of God is unconditional and amazing. There is no love that can be found anywhere on this earth that compares with the love of God. The love of God is the love that we were created to know. I wish there was some way I could adequately describe it in words.

Trading Loneliness for Peace

Another change in my life was something it took more than a year for me to notice. Before I received Jesus, every few months, it would occur to me that I was lonely. It didn't matter whether I had a girlfriend or how many parties I was going to or how many people I surrounded myself with, every few months, a feeling of loneliness would hit me. When I would feel the loneliness, I would call someone on the phone or smoke some pot in order to take away the feeling, but a few months later, it would hit me again. About a year and a half after becoming a follower of Jesus, I realized that I was no longer experiencing those periodic feelings of loneliness.

Over the last 30 years, I have not once had that feeling of loneliness. I think of the quote by Augustine that I read almost 40 years ago, "Oh, God, You have created us for Yourself, so that our hearts are restless until they find their rest in You." It wasn't a religion that changed my life. It was a relationship with the God who created the universe. And He gave me a peace that goes beyond my understanding (even in hard times).

I now believe that what they say is true, that every human being has a God shaped hole in their heart, and only God can fill it. We can try to fill it with the passing pleasures or riches of this life, but only God can fill a God shaped hole.

No sports, stuff, sex or success can compare to knowing God. Some people think, "If I was just rich or famous, or rich and famous." Money is a cold, heartless god. It doesn't bring peace. And suicide rates for famous people are higher than they are for the rest of us. They achieve their dreams and then think, "Is this all there is?" It's empty.

But the True and Living God can give us peace and joy that we can't find anywhere else.

And He wasn't done changing my life through powerful spiritual experiences.

7

The Voice of Thunder

About a year after becoming a follower of Jesus, I reached a crossroad in my life. I had bought out my business partner's half of our window cleaning business and my business was starting to grow. I was making a decent amount of money. Business was good. I had all the work I could handle. But the thought occurred to me that God was wanting me to be more involved in His work, and less interested in mine.

I was cleaning the windows of a house on Lanikai beach for a man who was starting a Christian television station in Tonga (in the South Pacific). I had been studying the Bible for about a year and had learned about some of the false teachings of cults like the Watchtower Society (whose members are known as Jehovah's Witnesses) and the Mormon church (also known as Latter Day Saints). The man asked me to pray about going to Tonga to help with the building of the TV station. He mentioned that there were lots of Mormons in Tonga who I could tell about the real Jesus.

I also had started to pray that God would put (as I termed it) a spearhead on my faith. I wanted to know for certain that the Bible is "the Word of God." I knew that Jesus had changed my life, but I wanted other pieces of my Christianity to come together.

I had been praying on and off about these three things (my work, going to Tonga and my faith) for about a week. One morning at about 4:30 AM, a voice spoke to me and woke me up. It said, "You've been asking for a sign. Here it is." At that moment, the loudest thunder I had ever heard, exploded directly overhead. Wow! I had been wanting a "spearhead" on my faith, but I hadn't thought I was asking for a sign, but when the voice spoke to me, I realized that indeed, that really was what I had been asking for.

I was renting a room (that was attached to a house) at the time. I got out of bed and walked out of my room and sat facing the swimming pool. It was raining lightly as I sat there praying, and I could see an occasional small flash of lightning off in the distance. Hawai'i has occasional thunderstorms but nothing like the ones on "the mainland" US. I was sitting there for just a few minutes when all of a sudden, the sky lit up above me. It was like a very bright flash of lightning, but it wasn't just white. It flashed from gold to white and then back to gold. At the exact instant of the flash, an extremely loud thunder exploded. I was flooded with a message from my head to my feet- "TIME IS SHORT!"

One of the amazing things about this was that the flash of light and the sound of thunder occurred at precisely the same instant. This was not like ordinary thunder, which you might hear several seconds after you see a flash of lightning.

There was no sense of what "short" meant. Was it a week, or 50 years? I don't know, but there was an urgency to it, "TIME IS SHORT!"

That was it. My decision was made. I would sell my window cleaning business and go to Tonga as a missionary to help start the Christian TV station. If time is short, I need to be living 100% for God and His purposes.

About 20 seconds later, another bright flash of light lit up the sky in the same place as the first flash of light, directly above (and slightly in front of) me- gold to white to gold again. At that same instant there was another explosion of thunder and another message shot through me from my head to my toes. Every fiber of my being was filled with the message- "God is a God of wrath!" I knew that God is a God of love and incredible mercy. He has forgiven me for every single sinful thought I'd ever had and sinful action I had ever done (and will do). He is so loving and merciful.

If there is one thing I have learned more than any other thing in my almost 30 years of following Jesus; it is that God loves us. But I had thought that since He is so loving, maybe He would forgive everyone's sins. I knew that people knew they were sinning, but I figured they didn't really know how serious it is. Maybe God would just forgive everyone.

That second message instantly cleared things up for me. Yes, God is a God of incredible love and mercy, but He is also a God of absolute justice and righteousness. He is a God of absolute righteous indignation. (Would a truly good God allow mass murderers and rapists to go unpunished? How about those who are murderous at heart?) He will execute absolute justice for every single sin that every person has ever committed. (But the Bible teaches that for those who put their trust in Jesus, God's wrath has already been poured out on Jesus, for our sake.)

The power and sense of God's wrath is not something I can fully communicate, but as a very meager representation, I will share an idea that came to mind. Imagine (what some call) a "potato bug" (also known as a roly poly bug or a pill bug) standing on an iron anvil, lifting up a clenched fist toward Heaven and defiantly shouting with its puny little voice, "You're not going to tell me what to do!" And then picture a mountain slamming down on that bug. Like I said, I can't perfectly describe the amount of wrath and power that will be poured out, but I think this somewhat communicates the idea.

About 20 seconds later, from the same spot in the sky- directly overhead (slightly in front) of me, the sky flashed gold to white to gold again. That same instant, another very loud thunder exploded, and I was filled with a third message. The message was that the United States would go to war with Iraq. That was January 9th, 1991- seven days before the US invaded Kuwait (to drive out the Iraqi military). Up to that point, I didn't believe the US would really go to war with Iraq.

You might wonder why God would tell me that in advance of it happening. There are several times in the Bible where it reports of God giving someone a message and then in effect saying, "This is how you will know that I have spoken to you. I am telling you the future in advance, so that when it takes place, you will know that I have spoken to you." I believe God spoke to me with a voice of thunder and told me those three messages. The third one was to help prove to me that it really was God who had spoken to me. He told me the future in advance.

Like Thunder Over the Waters

About nine months later as I was reading the Bible, I read a verse that I had never read before, "The voice of the LORD is over the waters; The God of glory thunders;"[1] I was amazed again. God had spoken to me months earlier with a voice of thunder; a voice that came from the sky directly in front of and above me, as I sat facing a swimming pool. Truly, there are times when God's voice thunders "over the waters."

Since that time, God has not spoken to me with a voice of thunder. I am just a regular follower of Jesus. But for the past 30 years, God has been speaking to me and guiding me every day, usually through the Bible and through the "still small voice" of His Spirit.[2]

---

[1] Psalm 92:3
[2] 1 Kings 19:12

I will not take the time now to share about all the ways that God has clearly guided and greatly blessed me, since becoming a follower of Jesus 30 years ago. (I have shared some of them in my other books.) But let me briefly say that not only does God speak to me (and want to speak to you) daily, He uses me (and wants to use you) to bless people for His loving, eternal purposes.

God has also worked miraculously in my life. And just like the healings written about in the Bible, God has instantly healed me (on three different occasions) of a potentially fatal disease. I have seen Him do miracles in healing others in response to prayer. He quite often tells me the future in advance, and I've heard from many others, how He has told them the future in advance as well. Nothing He has ever told me has been wrong. And no prediction of the future has been wrong either. He is real and alive, and I can confidently say that real Christianity is not about religion. Far from it; it's about a relationship; a personal relationship with the creator and sustainer of the universe. People who think Christianity is just a matter of believing in God, like someone might believe in Santa Claus or the tooth fairy, has no idea what real Christianity is.

If someone was to ask me if I am a Christian, I would want to ask, "What do you mean by the word 'Christian?'" There have been many people killed and mistreated in the name of religions of the world, and "Christianity" is one of those religions. Many people think of "Christians" as people who are hypocritical and judgmental. I don't know if the world needs more of what many people think of as "Christians," but I believe the world would benefit greatly from having more people who are followers of Jesus.

Says Who?

My life had been changed dramatically by a personal encounter with Jesus Christ. It wasn't religion. It wasn't a sales pitch I had fallen for. And it wasn't about going to church, even though I was now attending a church that was a great joy to be a part of. Every time I go to church, I am surrounded by people who have had their lives changed by entering into a personal relationship with Jesus Christ- people like me (and of course, some of them have not received Jesus yet, but they are checking this "Jesus stuff" out).

Every one of them has a unique story, but in every person's story that I hear, it comes down to a point of them personally asking Jesus to forgive their sins and to be their Lord and Savior. None of them "joined a religion." None of them were talked into joining "a church." God has worked in every life in such unique ways in order to bring them to that place of deciding to follow Jesus. God Himself has radically changed their lives.

It is also amazing that the people who have decided to follow Jesus are so often, very different from each other. People usually hang out with people who they have a lot in common with. But I have a friend who is a nuclear physicist and have several friends who are engineers. I know lawyers (yes, even lawyers can get right with God), doctors, nurses, teachers, former drug addicts and people who have never taken an illegal substance, surfers, people young and old, single mothers, multi-millionaires and people who are unemployed, people who have PHDs and high school dropouts. I've met Christians from numerous other countries who come from completely different cultures and when I meet them, it somehow seems like I've known them for years. And for the most part, we all get along great! It's amazing. (And it's not because someone got us all to drink the same Kool-Aid!)

Can We Trust That Book?

A reasonable question came to my mind after becoming a follower of Jesus, "Ok, so my life has been changed by Jesus. But what about the Bible? Is it trustworthy?" I had heard that it was sort of like the game of postman that I had played as a kid. A bunch of people sit in a circle and one person whispers a message into the ear of the person next to them. That person then whispers into the ear of the person next to them, and so on around the circle. Once the message goes all the way around the circle, the last person to hear the message and the first person to whisper it, speak the message out loud. The message has usually changed dramatically from what was whispered by the first person in the circle.

The Bible was written and then copied by hand and as those manuscripts were wearing out, they'd be copied. This happened over and over and now it is 2,000-3,000 years later. According to some people, the message of the Bible has dramatically changed. Is that true? I needed to know.

Another question that ties into that question: Did God write the Bible or was it written by some people who had nothing better to do than to make up a bunch of stories? Being the skeptic that I am, I needed to know. The last thing I wanted to do was to take people's word for it and fall for a bunch of lies that had been repeated so many times, to so many people, that it had become widely accepted as true. I needed proof!

8

Evidence

I started checking out the evidence for myself. One of the books that I read that was a great help was a book by Josh McDowell, titled, *Evidence that Demands a Verdict*. The book lays out a great deal of evidence. For example, there are "Old Testament" manuscripts of the Bible (some were written hundreds of years before Jesus was born) called the Dead Sea Scrolls, that were put into clay jars in the Qumran caves in Israel (around the time of Christ) and had sat there for about 2,000 years.

In 1947, some shepherds found them by accident. Amazingly, the manuscripts are almost identical to the manuscripts that our modern Bibles were translated from. The few differences were "obvious slips of the pen or variations in spelling."[1] Thousands of years of transmission (copying one manuscript to another as the older manuscripts wore out) without change? How could that be?

The Jewish people believed the Scriptures were "the Word of God" and when a manuscript was wearing out, they went to great lengths to make sure they were accurately copied. For example, they would count every letter and every word, and record in the margins such things as the middle letter and word of the manuscript. It would then be compared with the manuscript it was copied from. If a single error was found, the copy was immediately destroyed.

---

[1] Gleason Archer, Jr., A Survey of Old Testament Introduction, 1974, pg 25.

The "New Testament" manuscripts (written after Jesus died and rose from the dead) are also amazingly well preserved. The New Testament manuscript evidence is very impressive, with 24,000 known copies, more than 5,000 of which are complete (they include the entire New Testament). Some date as early as the second and third centuries A.D.

In 70AD (within just a few years of most of the New Testament being written), when Jerusalem was attacked by Roman soldiers, Jewish Christians fled to a number of other countries. They lived in these countries and now, almost 2,000 years later, manuscripts from these different countries have been found and compared and they too, are almost identical to each other.

What this tells us is that the Bible hasn't changed from when it was first written. (For more support for this claim, I highly recommend the books, *Evidence that Demands a Verdict*, by Josh McDowell, and *A General Introduction to the Bible*, by Norman Geisler and William Nix.)

So What? Who Says God Wrote the Bible?

You might ask, "But what if we find a comic book that has been copied from other comic book manuscripts dating back to 2,000 to 3,000 years ago? The fact that it was originally written thousands of years ago and hasn't changed from its original writing, doesn't make it true." That's right. It doesn't. So, we need to look at more evidence. Archeological evidence is of some value in this regard. There are archeologists in the middle east who are atheists (they don't believe God exists) but they use the Bible to guide them in archeological exploration. Why? Because the Bible is so accurate when it comes to its reporting about everything from kings to coins, and from cities to settlements, etc.

There are many times when critics will try to fault the Bible by claiming that certain kings or cities (etc.) mentioned in the Bible; never existed. Over and over they have been proven wrong by the archeologists. Many thousands of archeological discoveries have supported the claims of the Bible. And hundreds of cities mentioned in the Bible have been verified by archeologists.

There are other books that claim to be written by the guidance of God that we can compare in this regard. Take, for example, the Book of Mormon. The author, Joseph Smith, claimed that the Book of Mormon was "the most correct of any book on earth."[2] And yet even Mormon Archeologists admit that there is no archeological support for the things talked about in the Book of Mormon. Not one city. Not one coin. Things that the Book of Mormon says existed 2,000 years ago in America include metal swords and breastplates, gold and silver coinage, and even machinery; barley, wheat, donkeys, cows, goats, sheep, horses, oxen, swine, and elephants... even a battle on "Hill Cumorah" in upstate New York where supposedly over two million people were killed. There is not a shred of archeological evidence that any of these things existed in ancient America.

Many of the events in the Book of Mormon supposedly took place after Jesus rose from the dead (around 32AD). While thousands of archeological discoveries support Biblical claims (some dating thousands of years before Christ), there has not been a single archeological discovery that supports the Book of Mormon's claims; nor any DNA evidence to support the Book of Mormon's claims that native Americans are

---

[2] Book of Mormon, Introduction; Joseph Smith, *History of the Church*, 4:461

descendent from a "lost tribe" of Jewish people who allegedly migrated from Israel to America.

Mormon Anthropologist, Dr. Tom Murphy says, "The Book of Mormon is factually wrong. It gets the wrong plants. It gets the wrong animals. It gets the wrong technology. It's got the wrong languages. And it's got the wrong culture."[3] And as Mormon Anthropologist William Wilson said, "... the chance of the Book of Mormon being true is zero... The Book of Mormon is 19th Century religious fiction."[4]

But you might rightly say, "Just because the writers of the Bible are historically accurate, it doesn't prove that the claims about God and other things (like miracles) are accurate. Like a modern novel writer, the writers of the Bible could have taken historical facts and combined them with mythology and story-telling." That's right, so we need to look at more evidence to prove whether or not the Bible is true.

This is where the strongest evidence of Divine authorship is worth considering; prophecy (predictions of the future). In the Bible, God says "I am God, and there is no other; I am God, and there is none like Me, declaring the end from the beginning, and from ancient times things that are not yet done."[5]

Telling the Future

God in effect says, "This is how you will know that I wrote this book. I will tell you the future in advance." In fact, the Bible gives the test of a false prophet. It says that if a prophet makes one prophecy that doesn't happen as predicted, the prophet is a false prophet.[6] (If there is a

---

[3] The Bible Vs. The Book of Mormon, Video by Living Hope Ministries, Brigham city, UT, 2000
[4] Ibid.
[5] Isaiah 46:9-10
[6] Deuteronomy 18:20-22

God who knows everything, how could He possibly make a mistake?!) If the Bible makes one false prophecy, we can reject it as false and throw the whole thing out! While many psychics and fortune tellers claim to be able to predict future events, have any of them even been close to 100% accurate in their predictions? No. None of them have been right in more than just a fraction of their predictions. But the Bible has been right in every single prediction.

Almost a third of the verses in the Bible are prophetic- they tell the future in advance. There are about 2,500 predictions made in the Bible. That's a lot of predictions. Since the Bible was written by 40 different authors over a period of 1,500 years, if the Bible writers weren't directly guided by an all-knowing God, it should be very easy to find places where these writers contradict each other (it would seem that 40 different authors, writing over a 1,500 year period of time, no matter what the subject matter is, would not all agree with each other about everything they write about). But there aren't any contradictions in the Bible. (For more on this, read *Alleged Discrepancies of the Bible* by John Haley, or *Encyclopedia of Bible Difficulties* by Gleason Archer.)

And even more significantly, if God didn't guide the writing of the Bible, there should be many prophecies that were made, that didn't come true. There aren't. There isn't one single prophecy in the Bible that hasn't been fulfilled exactly as predicted, other than the (approximately) 500 prophecies that have not yet been fulfilled. These 500 prophecies pertain to things that are still in the future, for example, prophecies concerning the return of Jesus Christ and the soon coming one-world government, a one-world religion and a one-world leader.

There are many prominent people (including former President George Bush) who have talked about "a new world order" and many people are working toward a global religion.

There is already a European Union (with its European Defense Union military arm) and an African Union. It is not far-fetched to imagine a soon coming Global Union of some sort (or at least a strengthened United Nations) with a single leader.

In his book, *Earth in the Balance*, former US Vice President Al Gore lists what he thinks are the world's major problems and then presents what he thinks are the solutions: a one world government and a one world religion. Those are the very same things that the Bible predicts will be instituted by a world leader who the Bible calls the antichrist (a.k.a.- "the beast") in the last days.[7]

The Mark of the Beast

In fact, the Bible prophecies that the antichrist will require everyone "to receive a mark on their right hand or on their foreheads, and that no one may buy or sell except one who has the mark..."[8] It goes on to say that the mark of the beast is associated with the number 666.[9]

What makes this prophecy amazing to us living today is that (almost) every product sold in retail stores in more than 160 countries (of the world's 195 countries) has a Universal Product Code (UPC) on it. The UPC is a bar code that is read by a scanner when you buy things at the store. There are two thin longer lines at the beginning, the middle and the end of that bar code (take

---

[7] Revelation 13
[8] Revelation 13:16-17
[9] Revelation 13:18

a look). They are the image of the number "6" in computer code.

The scanner locks onto the 666 and reads the numbers in between them to get pricing and other product information. Microchip implants (that do not have the number 666 in them) are now being put in pets and even into people for the sake of convenience and security. It is easy to imagine a time when world leaders will require that every person take a microchip implant.

People could easily be tracked by satellites or drones. And this type of technology (RFID, etc.) already exists and is being used in credit cards, drivers' licenses and passports. These chips are used to track employees, patients, students, prisoners, animals and more.

World leaders could easily justify such an invasion of privacy by citing the benefits of these implants. The number of terrorist attacks could be greatly reduced as culprits are quickly tracked and eliminated from society.

It could help stop the spread of infectious diseases, prevent kidnapping and tax fraud and would be useful in so many other ways. It could be part of a cashless society. Nobody would need to carry cash or credit cards (or fear having them stolen) since all monetary transactions could be performed electronically.

The Bible's prophecy of people around the world not being able to buy or sell without having a mark on their hand, must have sounded far-fetched 2,000 years ago when it was written. But the prediction that people won't be able to "buy or sell" without a number (even the number 666) on their "right hand or forehead" does not sound far-fetched now.

Technologies are changing quickly so we don't know exactly what it will look like, but we know that one day in the not too distant future, people will be required to take a mark on their right hand or forehead. And it will be associated with the number 666. Without it, people won't be able to buy or sell. It will be used by the antichrist to control people. Whatever you do, don't take that mark![10]

Other Prophets

It's amazing that 2,000 of the Bible's prophecies have already been fulfilled exactly as predicted. But what about other "prophets" that have foretold the future?

Nostradamus is a well-known name when it comes to prophecy. A lot of people believe he has made many predictions that have come true. But a very brief examination of his prophecies quickly shows him to be a false prophet. For example, many people think he predicted Adolf Hitler's rise to prominence. In fact, however, the prophecy Nostradamus made that supposedly predicts Adolph Hitler mentions "Hister," not Hitler. People say it's a misspelling of Hitler's name.

But not only are the spelling and predictions about "Hister" inaccurate in describing Adolph Hitler; "Hister" is the Latin word for the Danube river. Nostradamus was talking about a river, not a future leader in Germany. (A brief examination of Nostradamus' prophecies reveals many false prophecies such as this one.) There is no comparison between false prophets like Nostradamus, Edgar Cayce, Jean Dixon, Joseph Smith (founder of the Mormon cult) and Charles Taze Russell (founder of the Watchtower Society cult); and the writers of the Bible.

Neither the Quran, the Hindu Vedas, the Buddhist Sutras, the Book of Mormon, the Watchtower Society's "New World Translation of the Holy Scriptures," the writings of Confucius, Mao Tse-Tung, nor any other book or writing compares with the Bible.

As God says, "... who can proclaim as I do? Then let him declare it and set it in order for Me,"[11]

---

[10] Revelation 14:9-11
[11] Isaiah 44:7

A few of the more amazing predictions of the Bible that have been fulfilled in recent years-

Israel would be dispersed and then be regathered as a nation. In the Bible, God said, "Surely I will take the children of Israel from among the nations, wherever they have gone, and will gather them from every side and bring them into their own land; and I will make them one nation in the land, on the mountains of Israel."[12] Never in recorded history has a nation been dispersed for more than a few years, and then come back together as a nation. It would seem to be a strange prophecy if it hadn't actually been fulfilled.

The Jewish people were scattered all over the world just as the Bible predicted, but amazingly, they retained their identity as being Jewish for 2,000 years. Then the people of Israel began returning to their homeland and on May 14th, 1948, Israel again became a nation. Have you heard of any other nation being driven from their homeland but keeping their identity for thousands of years (or even hundreds of years)? No, because it hasn't happened. But God said it would happen, and it did- exactly as the Bible predicted.

In the 11th chapter of the Old Testament Book of Daniel, in just 35 verses, there are 135 prophecies. And those prophecies have been fulfilled so precisely that critics say the book must have been written after the prophecies were made. But the evidence proves otherwise. In fact, even if the critics' wrong (late) dating of the writing of the Book of Daniel was accurate, some of the most amazing prophecies of Daniel were fulfilled hundreds of years after the manuscripts of Daniel were written.[13]

---

[12] Ezekiel 37:21-22

[13] And the late dating of the book of Daniel cannot be accurate because the book of Daniel was already widely accepted as being Scripture, hundreds of years before Christ.

Some of the Bible's prophecies that were written thousands of years ago are being fulfilled in our lifetime. Nobody can possibly say that these prophecies were written after the predicted events occurred.

For example, speaking of the end times, God makes an amazing prophecy by saying, "And it shall happen in that day that I will make Jerusalem a very heavy stone for all peoples; all who would heave it away will surely be cut in pieces, though all nations of the earth are gathered against it."[14]

Israel, a nation that is just slightly larger than the state of New Jersey, is the subject of more United Nations condemnations than all the other nations on earth combined.

From 2012 through 2016, the United Nations General Assembly adopted a total of 123 resolutions criticizing countries; 103 of those 123 have been against one country. Guess which one. North Korea? China? Iran? Russia? Saudi Arabia? Sudan? Syria? Nope- Israel. A whopping 84% of the UN criticisms are against Israel.[15]

And how could someone thousands of years ago accurately predict that "Jerusalem would be a heavy stone for all peoples... though all the nations of the earth are gathered against it"? It's a small city in a very small nation. And yet, just as the Bible predicted, Jerusalem has indeed become "a very heavy stone for all peoples,"- and it may very well be the epicenter of the next major world war.

How could the writers of the Bible make thousands of perfectly accurate predictions like these without making one false prediction? They were able to make thousands of perfectly accurate predictions because as

---

[14] Zechariah 12:3
[15] https://www.unwatch.org/un-israel-key-statistics

the Bible says, the Bible "is given by inspiration of God."[16] Or (as it says literally in the original Greek), it is "God-breathed."

Hundreds of the Bible's prophecies are about Jesus Christ. Many of them were written around 800 years before He was born. Among other things, these prophecies predicted the small town of Jesus' birth,[17] the exact timing of Jesus being revealed as the Messiah and the timing of His death,[18] that He would have His hands and feet pierced[19] (a very strange prediction, considering the fact that crucifixion wasn't even invented until hundreds of years after the prophecy was made), that He would be rejected by His own people (the Jews),[20] that He would rise from the dead,[21] that He would make a worldwide impact,[22] and that He would bring salvation (forgiveness of sins) even to the non-Jewish people "to the ends of the earth."[23] And those are just a few of the hundreds of prophecies that were perfectly fulfilled by Jesus.

In fact, about 500 years before Jesus was even born, the exact day of His entry in the city of Jerusalem was predicted.[24]

After the Fact?

Some people might wonder if the prophecies about Jesus were written after the events occurred. That would be one way to explain the absolute accuracy of the

---

[16] 2 Timothy 3:16

[17] Micah 5:2; Matthew 2:1

[18] Daniel 9:24-26

[19] Psalm 22:16

[20] Isaiah 53; Psalm 118:22; Luke 20:17-19, John 5:16-18

[21] Psalm 16:8-11

[22] Micah 5:4

[23] Isaiah 49:6

[24] Daniel 9:24-25 (see- www.allaboutthejourney.org/prophecy-about-jesus.htm)

predictions. The Dead Sea Scrolls that contain predictions fulfilled by Jesus, have been dated (using paleographic, scribal and carbon 14 dating methods) to 335 to 100 BC. So, these manuscripts were written at least a hundred years before Jesus was born (although the original manuscripts were probably written during the time period of 600 to 1,000 years before Jesus was born). So, the prophecies could not possibly have been written "after the fact."

Of course, the most amazing prophecy about Jesus was that He would be killed and then rise from the dead.[25] This prediction was made at least 700 years before Jesus was born. And during His life, Jesus repeatedly told His followers that He would be killed and rise from the dead on the third day.[26]

Then on the morning of the third day after being killed, there He was again- as alive as ever. And you can be sure that Jesus wasn't limping around like a man who had been tortured and had the blood drained out his body (through His wrists, ankles and heart, etc.) and somehow been revived. People watched the public crucifixion of Jesus. They watched Him be horribly beaten, tortured and then bleed to death. And they watched Him be stabbed in the heart with a spear after He was dead.

Then, on the third day after being publicly crucified, Jesus was able to convince people that He had conquered death. He hadn't just "almost died from His injuries" and been revived somehow. He wasn't limping around with bandages all over His body. He conquered death! He was alive and well! Jesus walked the earth for almost a month and a half after He rose from the dead. People spent time with Him, touched Him, talked with

---

[25] Isaiah 53:3-6, 10; Psalm 16:10
[26] John 2:18-22; Matthew 12:39-40; Matthew 16:21

Him, and even sat down and ate food with Him. How do we know this?

People Willing to Die for a Lie?

Hundreds or thousands of people watched Jesus be crucified. They knew He was dead. And hundreds of people said they saw Him alive again. A lot of them would be persecuted and some were even killed because they wouldn't deny their claims that they saw Jesus alive after He was crucified. There were over 500 eyewitnesses who saw Jesus alive at the same time after He rose from the grave.[27] Even non-Christian historians that were alive in the time of Jesus reported about these things.

Would you be willing to be beaten, imprisoned and possibly even killed for something you know is a lie? Do you think other people would be willing to do that? Or do you think those 500 people were all just imagining the same things at the same time?

Why would Jesus' disciples (other than Judas, who betrayed Jesus, precisely as Jesus predicted he would) give up everything they had or could possibly ever have on this earth, to face an executioner's death? Certainly, nobody would do it for a lie, let alone 11 of the 12 disciples.[28]

Dr. Simon Greenleaf, the famous Professor of Law at Harvard University, produced the famous three-volume work, A Treatise on the Law of Evidence, that "is still considered the greatest single authority on evidence in the entire literature of legal procedure."[29] The U.S.

---

[27] 1 Corinthians 15:6

[28] John didn't die. Tertullian (2nd century) wrote that John was "plunged... into boiling oil" but there is no definitive evidence that it happened.

[29] Wilber Smith, *Therefore Stand* (Baker Book House, 1973), 423

judicial system today still relies on rules of evidence established by Greenleaf.

Dr. Greenleaf was not a Christian and used to speak against Christians when he taught law classes at Harvard. Some of his students challenged Dr. Greenleaf to take his three volumes on the Laws of Legal Evidence and apply the principles to the evidence for the resurrection of Jesus.

Dr. Greenleaf accepted their challenge and after examining the evidence for himself, he came to the conclusion that according to the laws of legal evidence used in courts of law, there is more evidence for the historical fact of the resurrection of Jesus Christ than for just about any other event in history. Writing about the testimony of the writers of the four Gospels (Matthew, Mark, Luke and John), Dr. Greenleaf concluded, "Either the men of Galilee were men of superlative wisdom, and extensive knowledge and experience, and of deeper skill in the arts of deception, than any and all others, before or after them, or they have truly stated the astonishing things which they saw and heard."[30]

Dr. Greenleaf, like so many thousands of others (including many scientists) who have set out to disprove Christianity, came to the conclusion that it is indeed, the truth.

The Bible is the only book written that stakes it's claim to truth on fulfilled prophecy and has thousands of fulfilled prophecies to prove that its author is God. God in effect says, "This is how you'll know I've written this book. I will tell you history in advance." And the thousands of prophecies in the Bible are not vague Nostradamus style prophecies. Many of them are stated very clearly. No other book passes the tests that the Bible

---

[30] Simon Greenleaf, *Testimony of the Evangelists* (reprint of the 1874 edition, Grand Rapids: Baker Book House, 1984), 53

does. (More evidence at- www.allaboutGod.com and www.gotquestions.org)

The Testimony of a Hostile Witness

Another testimony to the truthfulness of the Bible is the history of the Old Testament and the Jewish people. In a court of law, the testimony of a "hostile witness" can be a strong support in a legal case. If someone is "on the other side" of a legal battle, but they are willing to admit that certain things are true that support your case, it can add a lot of credibility to your position.

The Jewish people have been the guardians and custodians of the Old Testament Scriptures (the part of the Bible that was written hundreds of years before Jesus was born). Most of these Jewish people completely reject Jesus as being the Jewish Messiah. And yet the Scriptures that they have preserved and kept so well, are the very Scriptures that lay out the hundreds of prophecies that Jesus fulfilled so perfectly. Nobody can say that the Jewish people conspired to insert hundreds of prophecies into the Scriptures that Jesus fulfilled. They are "on the other side" of the case. They reject Jesus, so they would have no reason whatsoever for trying to "make Him look good," and yet their own Scriptures are those that so perfectly predict His coming.

All by Coincidence?

The manuscript evidence, the archeological evidence, the prophetic evidence and the statistical improbability of those prophecies being fulfilled by chance; all give overwhelming proof that the Bible was superintended by God.

Peter Stoner, Chairman of the Departments of Mathematics and Astronomy at Pasadena College, along with 600 students, looked at just eight specific prophecies about Jesus. They came up with very conservative probabilities for each one being fulfilled, and then considered the likelihood of someone fulfilling all eight of those prophecies by chance. The conclusion to their research was staggering. The prospect of anyone fulfilling those eight prophecies by chance was 1 in 10^{17} (1 in 100,000,000,000,000,000 or 1 in 100 quadrillion). If you were to take 100,000,000,000,000,000 silver dollars and lay them across the state of Texas, Texas would be two feet deep in silver dollars. If you were to then mark one of those silver dollars, blindfold a friend of yours, fly them across Texas in a helicopter a few feet off the ground and ask your friend to reach out and try to grab the marked silver dollar, what would the likelihood be of your friend grabbing the marked silver dollar on the first try? It would be the same as the likelihood of one man (born at the time Jesus was born) fulfilling just eight of the prophecies that Jesus fulfilled. But He fulfilled hundreds of prophecies. And 2,000 of the Bible's prophecies have been fulfilled- just as predicted. It wasn't by chance. It was God.

But now you might say, "Well, Strat. That's your truth. But my truth is different." If you are brave enough, let's look at that for a few minutes.

9

Your Truth

"Facts are stubborn things; and whatever may be our wishes, our inclinations, or the dictates of our passions, they cannot alter the state of facts and evidence:"

- John Adams, 2nd US President

I was excited about how God had so radically changed my life and how He had given me the sure hope of eternal life in Heaven. And I was also excited to tell others about Him, "It's so simple! You can go to Heaven too! It's a free gift! Just turn from your sins and receive Jesus as your Lord and Savior!" Boy, was I excited! And I started to tell people about my new discovery.

Most people, however, didn't share my excitement about the chance to receive Heaven as a free gift. In fact, when I tried to tell people about Jesus, they would often say something like, "I'm happy for you. You found your truth." On the surface, that seems like a very nice thing for them to say. I think in many cases, they certainly meant well. They have their beliefs and they are happy that I have mine. "Whatever makes me happy." But let's take a closer look at that logic.

For thousands of years, many people around the world believed the earth was flat. It has now been demonstrated quite conclusively that the earth is not flat. It is spherical (almost round) in shape. But some people still believe the world is flat. A recent survey of American adults revealed that only 66% of young adults aged 18-24 have "always believed the world is round."[1] While I would not try to force anyone to believe that the world is round, the truth is, the "flat earthers" are wrong.

For almost 2,000 years, even up to the late 19th century, the majority of doctors believed that "bloodletting" (the withdrawal of blood from a person), was the best way to prevent and cure illness. (It may be that President George Washington would have recovered from his case of strep throat, were it not for misguided doctors draining his blood, and sadly, he wouldn't be the only person who died needlessly from the practice of bloodletting.) In the 1930's and 40's, advertisements about "healthy" cigarettes were common (some of them featuring medical doctors). It is now estimated by the World Health Organization that more than 7 million people die every year from cigarette smoking.[2]

Sincerely Wrong

If you have a friend who in their quest to be healthy, regularly has large quantities of blood drained from their bodies and smokes several packs of cigarettes a day, and believes that it is smart and safe to drive blindfolded, going the wrong way on freeways at 90 miles per hour, would you say, "Well, whatever makes you happy. You have your truth about what leads to health and long life, and I have mine."? Or do you think it might be good to tell your friend that they are dangerously wrong and mistaken in their beliefs?

In the areas of science, mathematics and nutrition, truth is highly valued in our society. But it seems that truth regarding spirituality is vastly different. There seems to be an unspoken mythological belief held by

---

[1] https://today.yougov.com/topics/philosophy/articles-reports/2018/04/02/most-flat-earthers-consider-themselves-religious
[2] http://www.who.int/news-room/fact-sheets/detail/tobacco

many Americans that teaches that nobody can know what "truth" is when it comes to spiritual things. "How can anyone possibly know for sure?" It seems that in modern America, "truth" is highly subjective- we can each decide what "truth" is for ourselves. We can each have "our own" truth. But if someone doesn't believe in gravity and they walk off a cliff, does it matter how sincere they are? No, it doesn't matter how strongly they believe gravity doesn't exist. It doesn't matter how many other people share their belief that gravity doesn't exist. The truth will radically impact their life as soon as they take that last wrong step. You can have your own opinion, but you can't have your own truth.

What basis do we have for this modern mythology that we can all decide what is to be our own "truth"? Just because the majority of people believe something, does it make it true? Obviously not. The majority of doctors were wrong for almost 2,000 years about bloodletting, and millions of people were wrong in their beliefs about cigarettes being healthy, and the earth being flat. Majority opinion is not a valid measure of truth.

The evidence is overwhelming- the earth is round (spherical) and bloodletting is not the best way for people to stay healthy and cure illness. The evidence is also very conclusive that cigarette smoking is unhealthy, and so is driving blindfolded at 90 miles an hour going the wrong direction on the freeway.

Feelings Over Facts

We in 21st century America are now living in an age of feelings- "If it feels good, do it." People think, "How can someone else tell me what is right or true for me? This is my truth. You have no right trying to invalidate my truth." It used to be that truth was a foundation in people's lives. Now facts and truth seem to have been replaced by feelings- "Don't confuse me with the facts. I just want to live according to what I feel is true."

This is especially the case in the area of spiritual matters. One person may have feelings or experiences that seem to support the idea that there is no God. If there is no God (or afterlife), then we really don't need to be concerned about whether we do good or evil. Unless we get caught, we won't be held accountable for our actions and behavior in this life- we can do whatever we want. There will be no consequences after this life.

Some people think it doesn't matter what a person believes, as long as they "try to live a good life." Others think there is some form of universal consciousness and that as long as our good deeds outweigh our bad deeds, we will be ok in the afterlife. Others think that after we die, we will be reincarnated- that we'll come back over and over again in life after life, and if we don't get it right in this life, it's no big deal, we've got lots more lives to learn from and we'll eventually get it right. "Do a good deed or commit murder, it's all going to help us to learn as we progress along life's evolutionary path."

Others believe that when a person dies, they simply cease to exist. They believe that people have no spirit or soul that lives on after death.

Thinking it Through

The reality is that most people never think through the conclusions they have arrived at in regard to spiritual truth. "I'm going to come back as a dolphin or a bird." Really? How do you know that? What do you base that "truth" on? How do you know you won't come back as a virus, a slug or a dung beetle? How do you know you'll have another life? How do you know you'll come back at all? Do you have evidence for your beliefs? If so, how strong is that evidence? Is it strong enough to risk your eternal future on?

What evidence do you have to support the idea that if you make some kind of an effort in this life to "be good," you will be ok in the afterlife? Or that you will go to Heaven or come back in a better life next time if your good deeds outweigh your bad deeds? Or if you believe that "good" people go to heaven when they die, what evidence do you have to support that belief? How good do you need to be to get to heaven? And how do you know that?

Every time you sit down on a chair, you probably don't think, "I wonder if this chair will collapse on the floor." Why not? Because you've had lots of evidence to support the idea that chairs can be trusted. After all, you've probably sat on chairs thousands of times, and rarely had one collapse under you- at least not a chair that looked strong enough to support you. You have a reasonable amount of evidence to support your beliefs about chairs. But how much evidence do you have to support your beliefs about your eternal destiny? More evidence than you have for the trustworthiness of a chair?

Obviously, eternity is a very, very long time to be wrong. If there are two buses and one is going to go to the beach and the other is going to drive off a cliff, would you climb on one of them, hoping it's the bus that is going to the beach? Probably not. You would most likely want to make sure that you were getting on the "right" bus. Or you might not be willing to get on either bus! You might not want to take a chance like that. You would first want enough evidence to convince you that you are making the right decision before getting on one of the buses.

As I shared earlier, I had some "evidence" to support the idea that my beliefs about spirituality were true. It seemed believable enough. A spirit told me something in the Hawai'ian language that I didn't understand. I looked up the translation and found out that the message spoken to me described an event that I hadn't known had even happened (until I was told about the event later). After an out-of-body experience, I drew an almost perfectly accurate sketch (other than the mirror image component) of a custom-built house that I had never seen with my physical eyes and was told by the person who lived in the house that I had come into their kitchen. She described the exact same event that I had experienced. I saw what I thought were UFO's and someone who was with me described seeing the exact same thing at the same time. I experienced phenomena associated with the "harmonic convergence" that I hadn't even read or heard about, previous to my experiencing them.

This all seemed to be evidence that my spiritual beliefs were true. In time however, I was presented with far more compelling evidence that proved to me that I had been lied to; that the spiritual forces communicating with me were deceptive. Just because something is spiritual in nature, does not make it true.

Better than "My Truth"

As I have shared in this book, I have discovered truth. But it is truth that is far, far more compelling than anything I had decided upon to be "my truth." What has been revealed to me (and to you) is THE truth. God has given us a tremendous amount of evidence to prove to us that it is truth. And it hasn't just been revealed to me. It has been revealed to billions of people through the centuries. And that truth is what we all need. The evidence for it is overwhelming; absolutely trustworthy and convincing to anyone who is open to examining it. We could never figure out God on our own. As the Bible says, "Oh, the depth of the riches both of the wisdom and knowledge of God! How unsearchable are His judgments and His ways past finding out!"[3] But He says, "You will seek me and find me when you seek me with all your heart."[4] We can't figure God out, but we can open our hearts to receiving Him and He will reveal Himself to us.

It really is a matter of the heart. You can have some intellectual reasons why you don't want to believe in God, but I can assure you, your reasons are not valid. God is love and He is good. God is perfect. He created everything that is good because He is love. You can hold onto reasons why you don't want to surrender to Him, or right now, you can humble yourself and fully surrender to the God who truly is love.

When I take my last breath, I know with absolute certainty, that I will be ushered into the presence of God, into a place that has been described in the Bible; "Eye has not seen, nor ear heard, nor have entered into the heart of man the things which God has prepared for those who love Him."[5] We can't even imagine how good heaven will be. It will be so far above and beyond the best moments we have ever experienced in this life.

No Tears, Death, Taxes or Dentist Appointments

Heaven is a real place. Many people like to think Heaven is either a state of mind, or an emotional state of bliss. It's not. Heaven is a place, just like New Jersey and London are places, except that New Jersey and London won't last forever. Heaven will.

Right before Jesus left the earth, He said to His followers, "In My Father's house are many mansions; if it were not so, I would have told you. I go to prepare a place for you. And if I go and prepare a place for you, I will come again and receive you to Myself; that where I

---

[3] Romans 11:33
[4] Jeremiah 29:13
[5] 1 Corinthians 2:9

am, there you may be also."⁶ He didn't say, "I go to prepare a state of mind." He said, "I go to prepare a place." Heaven is a place.

Notice also that Jesus didn't just say, "I go to prepare a place." He said, "I go to prepare a place for you." God knows every single thing there is to know about you and He's preparing (or has already finished preparing) a place especially for you, because He loves you. Jesus didn't say, "I go to prepare a place and I hope you are ok with it." It's not like when you go into someone's house and see their wall colors and say, "Wow. I would never want to live in a house with purple walls." No. The place Jesus is preparing is designed just for you. As He said, in His Father's house are many "mansions." That word could also be translated as "dwelling places." Does that mean we each get our own mansion or bedroom in Heaven? The Bible doesn't say, but we know God has designed these many dwelling places with each of us in mind. We've seen what people can design and build but they are nothing in comparison to the awesome beauty of what God is preparing for us.

The Bible tells us that Abraham "waited for the city which has foundations, whose builder and maker is God."⁷ During his life, Abraham was not just looking forward to finding a wonderful state of mind; he was waiting and looking forward to going to a Heavenly city that God has designed and built. What God has prepared for us is not just "heaven on earth," it's a real place where we can go. It could be said that Heaven is more "real" than the earth. Everything you see on earth is temporary. Heaven is eternal. So, what is Heaven really like?

---

⁶ John 14:2-3
⁷ Hebrews 11:10

10

A Place Like No Other

We don't know exactly what eternity in Heaven will be like, but we can know some things about Heaven. The Bible says, "And God will wipe away every tear from their eyes; there shall be no more death, nor sorrow, nor crying. There shall be no more pain, for the former things have passed away."[1] There are many, many wonderful things about Heaven. For one thing, Heaven is a place of absolute comfort. We may experience a lot of emotional pain in this life. Sometimes we are healed from the pain we suffer. Sometimes we may be hurt deeply and not experience a complete healing from the wounds- but we will be completely healed in Heaven. We may have regrets about things we've done (or not done) in this life. In Heaven, we will be comforted.[2]

Will there be crying in Heaven? If there is, it will only be for a moment. We'll leave our tears at the door. Every tear that we cry for anything will be wiped away by God Himself.[3] An angel won't wipe away our tears- God will. We won't walk through a machine with an automatic tear wiper. And God won't just wipe away some of our tears- He will wipe away every tear. What could we be sad about? Maybe we'll be grieving from things we had suffered on the earth. He will wipe away every tear. Maybe we will be sorry that we didn't live a

---

[1] Revelation 21:4
[2] Luke 16:25
[3] Revelation 7:17

life that was worthy of Him. Maybe we'll be grieving about people who didn't make it to Heaven. It doesn't matter what the source of our sorrow may be- He will wipe away every tear. He is the "God of all comfort."[4] There will be no sorrow.[5] Isn't that awesome? You will have no sadness about anything, ever again. In Heaven, God Himself will comfort you with His perfect comfort.

There will be no pain in Heaven.[6] I can't wait. I sometimes joke when people ask me if I have any allergies. I say, "Yes, I'm allergic to pain." I am looking forward to being in that place where there is absolutely no pain.

No Sickness, No Death

Some of us suffer in this life from chronic illnesses. In Heaven, we will be healed.[7] There will be no sickness.[8] Isn't that awesome? There will be no heart disease, no cancer, no strokes, no diabetes, no arthritis, no Alzheimer's disease or dementia, no colds or flu, no pneumonia or coughs, no sore backs or achy joints, no cuts or bruises, no sprained ankles, no sores, no ear aches, no tooth aches, no trips or falls, no hospitals or doctors treating patients, no dentist appointments and no car accidents.

There will be no death.[9] That means we will not be getting old or decaying. We won't get wrinkles or age spots. Nobody will have dentures or crutches or wheelchairs or glasses. That is one of the wonderful things about Heaven- our bodies will never wear out. We will live forever!

---

[4] 2 Corinthians 1:3
[5] Revelation 21:4
[6] Revelation 21:4
[7] Revelation 22:2
[8] Isaiah 33:24
[9] Revelation 21:4

It all sounds so good. It's hard to imagine being free from all pain, sickness, sorrow, suffering and death. Does it sound too good to be true? It's no wonder that right after telling us about it, God reassures us by inserting a verse saying, "Write, for these words are true and faithful."[10]

All around us, we see things getting older and falling apart. Of course, it's not just our bodies that get old. Beautiful new cars get old, break down, rust and eventually end up in junk yards. Clothes wear out and end up in the trash. Houses wear out. Everything around us is getting older. Astronomers tell us that the entire universe is getting older and wearing out. It's suffering a slow death from heat loss. It's falling apart. Even the stars in the sky won't last forever- they're getting older. In fact, "the heavens" (the sky) and the earth will be destroyed by fire and God will make a new heaven (sky[11]) and earth.[12] The new earth and sky will never wear out. They will last forever.

The Ultimate Security

Most of us have material things we value. Whether they are houses, money, cars, clothes or other material possessions, they are always at risk. We can lose them either by natural disasters, fire, theft or simply by them wearing out, rusting, or being eaten by moths or termites. It won't be that way in Heaven. There is no rust in Heaven. Moths won't eat anyone's clothes.[13] Termites won't eat anyone's houses. People say, "Nothing lasts forever." Well, in Heaven, everything will last forever.

---

[10] Revelation 21:5

[11] The same Greek word is used in the Bible for Heaven and for the sky (the "heavens") although they are two different things. The context of the verses makes clear which meaning is intended.

[12] 2 Peter 3:7-13

[13] Matthew 6:20

You'll never have to worry about anyone stealing anything from you.[14] In fact, you won't worry about anything at all. There will be no burglaries, robberies or padlocks. There won't be any identity theft, and you won't ever lose anything. In Heaven, our treasures will be absolutely safe.

Heavenly Treasure, Treasurely Heaven

Not only will our treasures be safe in Heaven, but Heaven itself will be a treasure. It's beautiful beyond our wildest dreams. The descriptions of Heaven given in the Bible are so amazing, they are difficult to even imagine. When we look at a beautiful sunrise or sunset, or see the majesty of a clear, starry night, a beautiful mountain range or a powerful waterfall, we are in awe. The Bible tells us that "the heavens declare the glory of God."[15] The universe is an incredibly awesome place.

I took an astronomy class in college. It was there I began to grasp just how vast our universe is. Astronomers think there are between 200-400 billion stars in our Milky Way Galaxy and there are hundreds of billions of galaxies. It's estimated that the universe is more than 100 billion light years across. (One light year is about 5.8 trillion miles.) It's easy to get lost trying to comprehend just how big and magnificent the universe is. It's mind boggling. Looking at the images taken from the Hubble telescope is quite an experience. (You can see amazing images at: www.hubblesite.org) God's creation is amazing beyond description, and yet it doesn't compare to what Heaven will be like.

Things We Won't Have in Heaven

Heaven will be spectacular beyond our wildest dreams. And one of the many things we'll love about

---

[14] Matthew 6:20
[15] Psalm 19:1

Heaven, is what's not there. It's awesome that there will be no tears, death, sorrow, crying, pain, guilt, regrets, sickness, poverty, rust, moths, termites,[16] or theft.[17] Two of the things I am most looking forward to not being in Heaven are temptation and sin. As we are told in the book of Revelation- "But there shall by no means enter it anything that defiles, or causes an abomination or a lie."[18] When we get to Heaven, our true Home, we will never struggle again with the temptation to sin.

We will never be tempted to strike back at someone. We will never be tempted to be selfish, or lie, gossip, slander, lust or get angry. We will be in perfect peace.

Things We Will Have in Heaven

One thing we will have in Heaven, however, is joy. Many people have somehow gotten the idea that God is like a giant grumpy (or angry) old man sitting in Heaven, or that He (or "it") is some kind of massive energy field with no feelings. He is our Heavenly Father. We were created in His image.[19] The Bible says God "takes pleasure in His people."[20] He experiences pleasure. It won't just be people and angels that are joyful in Heaven. No, God Himself will be full of joy!

The Bible tells us that in God's presence is "fullness of joy."[21] When we get to Heaven, we will have joy beyond anything we have ever imagined. God is the God of joy- the creator and source of true joy. And God's desire is for every one of us to have fullness of joy; in this life and for eternity. As Jesus said, "These things I have

---

[16] At least they won't be destroying things- see Matthew 6:20
[17] Matthew 6:20
[18] Revelation 21:27
[19] Genesis 1:26-27
[20] Psalm 149:4
[21] Psalm 16:11

spoken to you, that My joy may remain in you, and that your joy may be full."[22]

Will You Be There?

The most important question in life for every one of us, is where we will spend eternity. It doesn't matter if you feel like you will go to Heaven, or whether or not you think you are a good person, or whether you have done more good deeds than bad deeds. What determines your eternal destiny, is what God says.

There are two types of people who get into Heaven: those who are perfect, and those who are forgiven.

How do we know that? We know it because the God who is true, the God who says in effect, "This is how you'll know that I've spoken to you. I will tell you the future in advance," (and then who gave us 2,000 prophecies of the future that have come true exactly as He said they would) is the one who has revealed it to us.

The Bible says, "it is appointed for men to die once, but after this the judgment."[23] Every one of us will face God on a day of judgment. People will have to give an account for every thought, word and deed that we have ever done. God is an absolutely loving God. In fact, the Bible says, "God is love,"[24] but God is also absolutely good, absolutely righteous and just. He is perfectly fair, and He will give every one of us what we deserve. Jesus lived a life that was perfect.[25] He deserved to go the Heaven.

But what do you and I deserve? Do we really want God to give us exactly what we deserve?

---

[22] John 15:11
[23] Hebrews 9:27
[24] 1 John 4:8
[25] Hebrews 4:15

Our Problem

Our problem is in this question- what do we really deserve? Do you deserve to Go to Heaven for eternity? Have you ever told a lie? (Come on, tell the truth.) We have all lied. That makes us liars. Have you ever been angry at anyone without a perfectly good reason? Ever? Jesus said, "You have heard that it was said to those of old, 'You shall not murder, and whoever murders will be in danger of the judgment.' But I say to you that whoever is angry with his brother without a cause shall be in danger of the judgment."[26] If you have been angry with someone without a perfectly good reason, it is as if you have committed murder in your heart. If you are driving down the road and someone cuts in front of you and you think, "Oh! I could kill that guy!" In your heart, you just killed him. Our problem is that we are all liars and murderers at heart.

"It's Fine as Long as You Don't Harm Anyone"

In the area of morality, a lot of people have adopted the mantra "Everything is fine as long as you don't hurt anyone else." Some people would add "including animals," to that phrase. The problem with putting our trust in that idea is that we all hurt others. Murdering people in our hearts may not seem like a big deal to us, but it is a big deal to the God who is perfectly good; who is perfect in justice and who will judge our every thought, word and deed.

Jesus said, "... I say to you that whoever looks at a woman to lust for her has already committed adultery with her in his heart."[27] Have you ever had strong sexual desires for anyone (that you aren't married to)? I have. That makes us adulterers at heart. Have you ever taken

---

[26] Mathew 5:21-22
[27] Matthew 5:28

anything that doesn't belong to you? (Even a paper clip?) I have. That makes us thieves.

If you, like me, have been guilty of these things, then you too are a liar, a thief, an adulterer and a murderer at heart, and we have only looked at four of God's 10 Commandments. Do you think liars, thieves, adulterers and murderers deserve to go to Heaven for eternity? Or do you think God will let them in just because He is nice?

"My God Wouldn't Judge Anyone"

It's common to hear people say things like, "My God wouldn't judge anyone." That of course is true if their god is just a figment of their imagination. But every one of us is going to have to stand before the real God who created the heavens and the earth. Imagine a murderer standing in a courtroom before a judge and defending himself by saying, "Well, yes, your Honor. I murdered those 10 people, but I have also helped elderly people cross the street. Secondly, I think you are a good judge, so I don't think you will hold me responsible for committing murder."

The judge might respond by saying something like, "You are right. I am a good judge. And that is exactly why I am going to see that justice is done. The fact that you did good deeds that you ought to have done, in no way takes away the fact that you have committed murder." God is good and loving and kind, but that in no way takes away from the truth that God is also a God of absolute justice. He will make sure that every single sin and wrongdoing is paid for. And as the Bible says, "all have sinned and fall short of the glory of God."[28]

The question is, who is going to pay your penalty? Are you? The Bible says "the cowardly, unbelieving, abominable, murderers, sexually immoral, sorcerers,

---

[28] Romans 3:23

idolaters, and all liars shall have their part in the lake which burns with fire and brimstone, which is the second death."[29] Do you want to stand before God on judgment day and be sentenced to a lake of fire, to pay for every single sinful thought and action you have ever committed? I sure don't. That's why it is so amazing that God is not only perfectly good and just and loving, but He is also merciful. As the Bible says, "the wages of sin is death, but the gift of God is eternal life in Christ Jesus our Lord."[30] God wants to give us the gift of eternal life.

The Perfect Gift

Jesus (who is God), took on human flesh and came to this earth, lived a perfect, sinless life and then was tortured and crucified for your sins and for mine. And God offers to place the penalty of our sins onto Jesus. It's a free gift.

The big question is; will you reject it or receive it?

The Bible says there are two things that are required to get into Heaven. The first is repentance. Repentance means "changing your mind" about your sins. It means that you choose to forsake those things that God says, are sinful. Secondly, you must put your trust in Jesus as your Lord and Savior.[31]

The Bible, speaking of Jesus, tells us, "But as many as received Him, to them He gave the right to become children of God."[32] If you will turn to God from your sins, and put your trust in Jesus Christ as your Lord and Savior, you will be saved from the judgment to come, be forgiven of your sins, and receive the free gift of eternal life in Heaven.

---

[29] Revelation 21:8
[30] Romans 6:23
[31] Mark 1:15
[32] John 1:12

You can choose to turn to God right now. If you want to have your sins forgiven and to receive the free gift of Heaven; right now, pray something like this- "Dear God, Please forgive me for my sins. Jesus, thank You for suffering and dying on the cross for my sins. Please come into my life and be my Lord and Savior. Help me to follow You. In Jesus' Name I pray, Amen."

I'm sorry if that sounds preachy or religious, but that's the simple truth. You and I will never be good enough to deserve Heaven, but the penalty for our sins has already been paid by the Son of God. All you need to do is to turn to God and receive His free gift of forgiveness.

"Earth is Good Enough for Me"

Some people might think, "Well, life on earth is good enough for me. I don't need to go to Heaven when I die. I think Heaven is on earth." For some people, life on earth is wonderful, but the truth is that you will go somewhere when you die. You will either go to a place that the God who created love, laughter, joy, beauty and peace; has created- Heaven; or if you reject God and His love and gift of mercy- you'll go to a place that God absolutely does not want anyone to go to[33]- a place where there is no love, no joy, no peace and no rest- a place where murders, liars and thieves (that's us) deserve to go- a place of torment.[34]

Nobody is Too Bad to Go to Heaven

Some people may think they are too sinful to possibly get through "the pearly gates." A man named Paul wrote one-third of the New Testament in the Bible. He is one of the best-known people in the whole Bible. Before he became a follower of Jesus, he hunted down

---

[33] 2 Peter 3:9
[34] Revelation 20:15

followers of Jesus, so he could beat them and put them in prison. He guarded the coats of the people who were killing the first Christian martyr.[35] God forgave him because he turned to God and received the free gift of forgiveness.

King David, a man who God calls "a man after My own heart"[36] was a man who committed adultery and murder. But God forgave David because he turned to Him and received the free gift of forgiveness.

You might think, "Well, I don't want to go to a place where people like Paul and David are. They are so evil. I'm a good person." Oh, but we've already looked at your heart and mine. None of us are too good to need God's mercy and none of us are so bad that God isn't offering it to us. We are all guilty. Some of us, more than others, but no one is good enough to deserve Heaven, "no, not one."[37]

And all you need to do to receive the free gift of eternal life in Heaven and to have a personal relationship with God, is to repent and receive Jesus as your Lord and savior.[38] Decide to put your trust in Him and believe that Jesus died for your sins and that He rose again on the third day.[39]

It's Not Rocket Science

Think about the scenario. God, who is love, is all-knowing and absolutely good. He created you for the purpose of knowing Him and of living a life that is pleasing to Him. And everything He wants for you is good, even though it may be very difficult at times. The God who created you and the rest of the universe is a God

---

[35] Acts 7:58
[36] Acts 13:22
[37] Romans 3:10
[38] John 1:12
[39] 1 Corinthians 15:1-4; Romans 10:9-13

of incredible love and mercy. He is also the God of absolute truth and justice. He is offering to give you the free gift of eternal life in Heaven. All you need to do is to turn to Him and receive it. Or, you can reject the purpose for which you were created. You can (like most people) reject the love and mercy of your Creator.

You can choose to live out your life (however long or short that may be) and then die and stand before God and be judged for every thought, word and action you have ever done. You will be found guilty and you will get exactly what you deserve. You will be in a place of torment- separated from God and all that is good, forever.

God loves you. He wants to forgive you. He wants to take you to Heaven forever. He wants you to know Him personally. Jesus said to the religious Israelite leaders, "O Jerusalem, Jerusalem, the one who kills the prophets and stones those who are sent to her! How often I wanted to gather your children together, as a hen gathers her chicks under her wings, but you were not willing!"[40] But you can soften your heart and say yes to God. Come to the God who loves you.

Experiences and Conclusions

Every one of us has our own set of experiences. We all come to our own conclusions based on a combination of past experiences, assumptions we have made (some of which may not be true) and things we have believed from the past (many of which, we may have accepted as true, but which may not actually be true). We often believe what we want to believe. Many people would rather believe a lie, than accept a truth that will result in them having to change the way they see the world or change the way they live their life.

---

[40] Matthew 23:37

But it doesn't matter what you have believed up to this point; if you haven't already put your trust in Jesus Christ, right now you can have your sins forgiven, you can have your life radically changed for the better and you can receive the free gift of eternal life in Heaven. God loves you so much. He is standing at the door of your heart, offering you the free gift of Heaven.[41] All you need to do is to receive it.

Jesus said, "... you shall know the truth, and the truth shall make you free."[42] As people, we should all seek to be tolerant of others. But truth itself is not tolerant. Gravity either exists or it doesn't. It is either healthy to smoke cigarettes, drive 90 MPH going the wrong way on the freeways, and have large amounts of blood drained out of our bodies to prevent and cure illness, or it isn't.

The reality is that it is true that driving blindfolded, going the wrong direction on the freeway is dangerous. It is also true that there is a God who created you, who loves you, and who wants you to know Him personally, to forgive every single sin you have ever committed, are committing and ever will commit, and who wants to take you to Heaven when you die. God really loves you. This is not true because I think it is. It is true because it is true. The God who created the universe says it is true in the Bible; the book that He wrote through people- a book like no other book ever written.

---

[41] Revelation 3:20
[42] John 8:32

11

Questions People Ask

There are some good questions that people ask when talking about God and Christianity. They are valid questions and knowing the answers can help people to understand what might otherwise seem confusing about God. I'll try to answer a few of them here-

How Could a Loving God Allow Suffering?

This is one of the most common questions people ask about God. If there is a God, and if this God is a God of love, then why would God allow suffering?

God is love.[1] And because God is love, He created humanity in a way that would allow each one of us to know His love and to love Him in return, as well as to love others. Love requires freedom of choice. If we were all created like robots- programmed to behave in certain ways, we couldn't love.

Let's say that we were to create a robot that was programmed to respond in a certain way to certain stimuli, and it said to you, "I-love-you," there would be something missing. It wouldn't be the same as if a human being was to sincerely choose to say, "I love you," because they really love you. Love requires the ability to choose.

Because God is love, He created us with the freedom to make choices- the freedom to love. As a result of people having the ability to make choices, people can choose to reject the God who loves them. They can

---

[1] 1 John 4:8

choose to love sin and hate God. When people choose to be prideful, greedy and selfish, there will be many choices that they make that will result in suffering for others and for themselves. The root cause of all suffering is sin. And the results of sin are devastating. But because God is love, He has decided to allow us to have freedom of choice, even though (for a time) there will be a lot of suffering as a result of humanity's choosing to sin. And as you know, not all of our suffering is a result of our own sin.

If a person decides to light their neighbor's house on fire, it can result in terrible consequences for their neighbor, for themselves, and for others as well. Sin can have ripple effects that go far beyond the person who commits the sin. But God has allowed us to have the ability to choose because He knows the value of love.

Love is so wonderful, that God is willing to allow sin and suffering for a time. From our perspectives, it may seem like the suffering on this earth has been going on for a long, long time. But as God tells us, "For what is your life? It is even a vapor that appears for a little time and then vanishes away."[2] As we looked at in this chapter, for those who choose to love God, the time of suffering will soon come to an end- forever. We will all be in Heaven where there will be absolutely no suffering- ever again.

God is willing to allow humanity's suffering for a season, in order to eternally bless those who choose to turn to Him.

Why Doesn't God Stop the Suffering?

He does. We probably have no idea how often and how much God has limited the suffering in our lives and in the lives of others. There are also many things that

---

[2] James 4:14

God has not allowed to happen- a worldwide nuclear holocaust, for example. There have been more than 125,000 nuclear weapons manufactured since World War II. I'm thankful that there has never been an accidental (or intentional) nuclear war started. Even 5, 10 or 100 nuclear weapons being launched accidentally could result in a major worldwide disaster. God has not allowed that to happen.

God has not allowed a terrorist to detonate a nuclear device (at least not yet) even though many thousands of them would like to do that. The International Atomic Energy Agency (IAEA) reported more than a hundred nuclear smuggling incidents between 1993 and 2006, eighteen of which involved highly enriched uranium, the key ingredient in an atomic bomb and the most dangerous product on the nuclear black market.[3] And we can be sure there have been many more nuclear smuggling incidents since 2006, but there hasn't been one terrorist nuclear attack (yet).

God has also not allowed there to be a global epidemic that would wipe out the human race (although it is estimated that as of the end of 2016, 35 million people have died from Aids-related illnesses [a disease which is often spread through behaviors which God tells us are sinful] and that 36.7 million people were living with HIV/AIDS, with 5,000 new infections per day).[4]

God has not allowed a large comet to strike the earth which could easily wipe out life on earth. God has not allowed atmospheric, weather or other cataclysmic events to occur that would wipe out the entire earth's population.

God only allows a certain amount of suffering and a certain amount of negative consequences to come from

[3] www.cfr.org/backgrounder/loose-nukes
[4] www.hiv.gov/hiv-basics/overview/data-and-trends/global-statistics

the actions of people. He may allow a lot more suffering than we think He should allow, but God would not be truly giving mankind the freedom to make choices, if God didn't allow the consequences of those choices.

As I mentioned earlier in this book, when my mother was eight years old, God allowed her father to die of a heart attack a few days after the attack on Pearl Harbor. Why? I don't know for sure, but I can see how God has worked over the last 77 years and what has now happened in my family. When my grandfather died, his family was doing very well financially. They lived in a beautiful home in an exclusive neighborhood in Hawai'i. If my grandfather had continued with his business ventures, I probably would have grown up in a very rich family. But I didn't. My divorced mother worked minimum wage jobs in order to provide for her four "little darlings" (as she called us).

If I was born and raised in a very wealthy family, I probably would have been even more prideful than I was by the time I reached the age of 30, when I asked Jesus to come into my life and forgive my sins. I may have been so proud that I may never have received Jesus.

But instead, not only did I receive the free gift of eternity in Heaven, but I have been a part of a number of people (including several of my relatives) entering into a personal relationship with Jesus. This includes my mother,[5] my grandmother, my uncle, and others. Was it worth decades of hardship for my family in order for there to be numerous people in Heaven for eternity?

When my family members and I are in Heaven, I believe we will thank God for allowing the suffering that He allowed in our family, since it was something He used

---

[5] Since my mother had Dementia, I realize that some might argue that she didn't know what she was doing when she prayed to receive the Lord.

in order to work things out for us all to eventually put our trust in Him.

As the Apostle Paul wrote, "And we know that all things work together for good to those who love God, to those who are the called according to His purpose."[6] God doesn't cause all things, but He does cause all things to work together for good to those who love Him. There is a big difference. God is not cruel. He is not a mean God. He does not intend for people to choose sin and its consequences. He does not enjoy allowing people to suffer. But He allows it and in the end, we will all see why. Sometimes when we are flat on our backs, all we can do is look up, and that can be a very, very good thing.

What About People Who Never Hear of Jesus?

How can a loving and fair God condemn anyone and not let them into Heaven, when they have never even heard of Jesus? The Bible tells us that "The heavens declare the glory of God; and the firmament (the sky) shows His handiwork. Day unto day utters speech, and night unto night reveals knowledge. There is no speech nor language where their voice is not heard. Their line has gone out through all the earth, and their words to the end of the world."[7] It also says, "since the creation of the world His invisible attributes are clearly seen, being understood by the things that are made, even His eternal power and Godhead, so that they are without excuse."[8]

God reveals certain things about Himself through creation. How can someone look at a beautiful sunset, a starry sky, a beautiful forest or a lake, (or the cuteness of a baby or young animal) and honestly think it all happened by random chance? We can't. The Bible also

---

[6] Romans 8:28
[7] Psalm 19:1-4
[8] Romans 1:20

tells us that God has given every one of us a conscience.[9] Cultures all around the world believe that murder is wrong. Is that because they all communicated with each other and entered into a mutual agreement? No, it's because God has put it in every person's conscience-murder is wrong. On the day of judgment, every person will be judged according to their conscience. And as we have looked at, we are all guilty of violating our consciences.

So, is everybody who hasn't heard of Jesus, going to Hell? God is all-powerful. He will not force Himself on you or on anyone, but He can intervene in people's lives and miraculously reveal Himself to them. As I shared about in my life story, I had absolutely no interest in Jesus. But He used a series of miraculous events to get my attention. He appeared to Moses[10] and the Apostle Paul miraculously[11] as well as to others in the Bible. And God can reveal Himself to anyone He wants to reveal Himself to in any way He wants to. In fact, many thousands of Muslims in the middle east are putting their faith in Jesus as a result of dreams and visions in which they say Jesus has revealed Himself to them.

You might say, "Well then, why doesn't God reveal Himself to me right now?" I believe God is revealing Himself to you right now, through this book. You might say, "No, I want to see God. Why won't He show Himself to me or perform a miracle to show me He is real?" God is gentle. He will not force Himself upon you, but God promises that if you whole heartedly seek Him, you will find Him.[12] God will be found by anyone who honestly seeks Him.

---

[9] Romans 2:14-16
[10] Exodus 3:1-4
[11] Acts 9:1-6
[12] Jeremiah 29:13-14

And the reality is, nobody comes to faith in Christ through a miracle. It might be part of the process, but the Bible says, "faith comes by hearing, and hearing by the word of God."[13] Even though God did (what I consider to be) miraculous things to get my attention, it wasn't until I heard the message of the Gospel (the good news) on the radio, that I received Jesus as my Lord and Savior. You don't need miracles in order to believe, you simply need to receive the message from God- the Gospel. God loves you. Jesus died for your sins and rose again on the third day. If you haven't received Jesus as your Lord and Savior, I suggest that before you become too concerned about the Pygmies in Africa who haven't heard of Jesus, that you make sure you have reserved your place in Heaven.

Why Have So Many Been Killed for Religion?

Many followers of religions through the ages have committed horrible atrocities. Religion has been used as an excuse for killing people. There is no denying this reality. Of course, there have been far more people killed by the atheistic Communistic regimes than by religious armies. It may be that as many as 100 million people have been killed as a result of Communism. That in no way diminishes what has been done in the name of religion however. One death is too many.

It's been estimated that as many as 1-3 million people were killed in the Crusades (which were reportedly carried out in order to reclaim land conquered by Muslims). It's important to realize that most of the atrocities committed by "Christians" in the name of Christianity weren't committed by Christians. A true Christian is a follower of Jesus. The Bible says, "you know that no murderer has eternal life abiding in him."[14]

---

[13] Romans 10:17
[14] 1 John 3:15

Nobody who is an "unrepentant" murderer is a follower of Jesus Christ.

While the Crusades were ordered and led by men who claimed to be Christian, in no sense should the Crusades be referred to as "Christian." Many Muslims in the middle east think that the American professional singer, Madonna, is a Christian because she wears crosses as jewelry, and many Muslims think that all Americans are Christians. It is highly unlikely that many of the participants in the Crusades really knew Jesus Christ as their Lord and Savior.

The Crusades were brutal and evil. Many people were forced to "convert" to "Christianity." If they refused, they were put to death. This is blatantly unbiblical. While the Bible gives support for the idea of being involved in a "just" war (stopping Hitler from taking over the world, for example), it does not condone killing anyone without a perfectly good reason. The Crusades may have been carried out by so-called Christians, but the actions that took place in the Crusades were absolutely contrary to all that the Christian faith stands for.

Who Are You to Judge Me?

I am nobody. I am not in a position to judge you. I can certainly understand why you might ask such a question as "Who do you think you are to judge me?" I am not God. I am not the determiner of what is right and what is wrong. It is not my place to judge. But there is someone who is in that place- God.

God created the universe. He gave you life. Your parents were involved but ultimately, since God created everything, He gave you life. In fact, when you consider the extreme complexity of the DNA code, you begin to realize how little your parents were responsible for your birth. And God created you for a purpose (a purpose that you are right now either embracing or rebelling against). So, God is in the position of being able to judge you. He knows everything and therefore He is in the place to be able to say what is right, what is wrong, what is good and what is evil.

I am not judging you. God's Word, the message from our Creator, is what judges us. The Bible is the "owner's manual" for our lives. It reveals that God loves you and created you for a specific purpose that He wants to fulfill in and through your life. But God is also the one who can say whether or not you are fulfilling that purpose. If a potter makes a jar of clay, he or she has the right to say whether the jar is cooperating with their creative hands.

The myth about truth being relative (what's truth for one person may not be truth for another) carries over into morality. People say, "Who are you to tell me what's right and what's wrong, what's good and what is not good? Who are you to judge me?"

The truth is that there is such a thing as good and bad; right and wrong. There are of course many situations in which something may be right for one person but wrong for another. For example, if a person runs into a crowded movie theater and shouts "Fire!", that's probably not a good thing. But if the theater is on fire, then maybe it would be a good thing.

But let's look at the bigger question; is there such a thing as absolute right and wrong; good and evil? Some people would say there isn't, and that we should each decide for ourselves what "good and bad" are and what "right and wrong" are. They would accuse us of being judgmental if we say certain things they do are wrong, bad or even "evil."

Using that standard (moral relativism), it would then be wrong to say that it was evil or wrong for Hitler to order the killing of millions of people, including Jews, Christians and homosexuals. "Who are you to judge

Hitler?" If there is no absolute right and wrong, if we can all decide on "our own truth," or if morality is determined differently in each culture, then we have no right to say that murdering millions of people is wrong.

At this point, people are quick to say that it is wrong to harm innocent people. Well, what if Hitler had ordered that all those people be killed gently, would it be ok? You might say, "But those people didn't want to die. It was therefore wrong of Hitler to kill them. He was forcing his will on others."

But what if Hitler was wanting to improve the human race? What if he was wanting to help humanity by improving the gene pool? Hitler was a strong believer in Darwinian evolution and like Charles Darwin, Adolf Hitler was extremely racist. What if he thought (as he implied in his writings) that billions of people would benefit in the future by having millions of people of "inferior races" killed by Nazism? He might say, "Who are you to judge me? I'm doing what seems right to me 'for an idealized future of our humanity.'"

The truth is that there is such a thing as right and wrong. Many people believe the modern myth- "There is no such thing as absolute truth." A quick look at that claim reveals that it is a self-contradicting statement and cannot possibly be true. It is a statement of absolute truth saying that there is no absolute truth. It is self-refuting. It's like saying, "It is an absoute truth that there is no such thing as absolute truth." It's nonsense and the statement contradicts itself.

On the other hand, if we have an absolute moral standard that teaches (for example) that murder is wrong, it changes everything. Then we can say with absolute certainty, that what Hitler did was wrong.

The God who created the universe and all of humanity, is perfectly good and all-knowing. And He has given us a book that tells us what is truly good and what isn't. We don't need to guess at it or try to figure out "our own truth" about what is right and wrong. We can read the owner's manual.

Don't All Religions Teach the Same Things?

Most religions teach a number of similar things. The idea of doing good to others is a theme that runs through a lot of the world religions. And I'm sure that almost everyone would agree that it is true that we should do good to others. This is a God given truth that is engrained in our consciences. We would probably all agree that there is some truth in most, if not all of the world's religions.

But there are many things that are contradictory between one religion and another. For example, Buddhism teaches that people are reincarnated. Christianity teaches that people live once, then die and are judged[15]- there is no such thing as reincarnation. People are either reincarnted or they aren't. They can't both be true.

In Buddhism, there is no belief in a personal God. Mormonism teaches that there are many gods, that God was once a man who progressed to become a God; that people can become gods and that Jesus is the spirit brother of Lucifer (the devil). The Watchtower Society (Jehovah's Witnesses) teaches that Jesus is not God but is Michael the archangel, a created being.

The Bible teaches that Jesus is God[16] and that "by Him all things were created that are in heaven and that are on earth, visible and invisible..."[17]

Again, all religions can't be true if they contradict each other.

---

[15] Hebrews 9:27

[16] John 1:1; John 20:28; Titus 2:13; Philippians 2:5-8; Hebrews 1:8; Revelation 1:17, 2:8, 22:13; Isaiah 7:14, 9:6; Matthew 1:23

[17] Colossians 1:16

But Jesus made some claims that contradict every other religion. He said, "I am the way, the truth, and the life. No one comes to the Father except through Me."[18] Jesus claimed that the only way to have a personal relationship with God is through Him. Every other religion would deny that this is true.

The question is: Is Jesus a liar, a lunatic, or the loving and true God, who took on a human flesh, came to this earth, lived a sinless life and then died on the cross for our sins? As they say, Jesus is either the Lord, a liar or a lunatic. You can't say that Jesus was just one of many "ascended masters." He was either telling the truth, He was crazy, or He was a liar.

People were willing to be beaten, tortured and killed, rather than deny their claims that they saw Jesus alive after he'd been crucified and raised from the dead. Truth was a big deal to the followers of Jesus. If these people who said they were eye-witnesses, were making stories up about what He said and did, surely they would have recanted rather than face death.

But even non-Christian historians give accounts of the suffering that early Christians were willing to endure rather than deny the words and works of Jesus. And there are thousands of ancient Bible manuscripts gathered from all over the middle east and they all say the same things.[19] So people can't cling to the convenient modern mythology of "Well, Jesus probably didn't really say all those things that people say He did."

There is an old story about a group of blind men who walk up to an elephant. Each man approached from a different direction and when they walked up to the elephant and touched it, each man's experience was different. The man who felt the tusk said, "An elephant

---

[18] John 14:6
[19] Other than a few spelling and other very insignificant differences.

is a long, hard, pointed thing." Another man felt the side of the elephant and said, "An elephant is like a wall." Each man gave a different description of what the elephant was like.

This is a very convenient story to help explain why different religions are different, and it can help explain why some very different beliefs exist about truth and religion. But the story breaks down when it comes to being true. While other religions may be attempts by people who really don't understand the truth, to come to the knowledge of truth (like blind men approaching an elephant), Christianity is very different. The God who created the universe has revealed Himself to humanity and has revealed a lot about what is true and what is false, about what is good and what is not good.

We are not like blind men groping in the dark, hoping to catch a glimpse of the truth of God. God has come to us and revealed Himself to us. The guesswork and blindness is taken away. For anyone who honestly seeks for God, He said He will be found.[20] God is not an elephant who needs to be groped for in the dark. He is our loving Creator who has revealed Himself to us; our loving Creator who is inviting us to know Him and to have a personal relationship with Him.

The question is, are you willing to accept it. Jesus said, "the light has come into the world, and men loved darkness rather than light, because their deeds were evil. For everyone practicing evil hates the light and does not come to the light, lest his deeds should be exposed."[21] Have you turned from your sins and put your trust in the true and living God whose love for you is so great that it can't even be fully comprehended?[22]

---

[20] Jeremiah 29:13
[21] John 3:19-20
[22] Ephesians 3:18

Do Christians Care About the Environment?

The Bible tells us that God created the earth and that we as people, are given the responsibility of caring for it. Describing the very beginning of humanity, the Bible says, "Then the LORD God took the man and put him in the garden of Eden to tend and keep it."[23] The idea is that people are given the responsibility by God to care for and cherish this wonderful planet. While many Christians care deeply about God's creation, it is also true that many Christians don't seem to care much about it. Why is that?

There are a few reasons. One is that Christians, like everyone else, were born with a selfish nature. While the goal is to allow God to work in our lives to make us better people, the reality is that we are all works in progress. As they say, "The Church is a hospital." We are all "sick" in some sense. Like children who are maturing, none of us have "arrived." None of us are all grown up yet.

God says, "I know all the birds of the mountains."[24] And Jesus said, "Are not five sparrows sold for two copper coins? And not one of them is forgotten before God."[25] The Bible tells us that God cares about the precious creation He has made. It is heartbreaking however, to see how little, some Christians care for the environment. God did not give the responsibility of caring for the earth, to animals. He gave it to people and it is sin for people not to take this stewardship responsibility seriously.

The reality of many Christians not caring a whole lot about the environment is magnified in many people's minds however, because many people do more than just care about the earth- they worship it.

---

[23] Genesis 2:15
[24] Psalm 50:11
[25] Luke 12:6

Many people worship the creation, rather than the Creator- the gift, rather than the Giver. In the Bible, the Apostle Paul writes about people who, "Professing to be wise, they became fools, and changed the glory of the incorruptible God into an image made like corruptible man—and birds and four-footed animals and creeping things. Therefore, God also gave them up to uncleanness, in the lusts of their hearts, ... who exchanged the truth of God for the lie, and worshiped and served the creature rather than the Creator, who is blessed forever."[26]

We were all created to know God and to love God. Many of us however, would rather not turn from our sin in order to love the God who loves us. Instead, we "changed the glory of the incorruptible God into an image." We love and worship the beautiful and wonderful creation that God has made, but we refuse to acknowledge God as God, or to give Him thanks for how He has blessed us.[27] It's like a loving parent who returns home from the store with arms full of gifts for their children. When the children look through the window and see the parent walking up to the front door, they run to the door and open it, grab the gifts out of their parent's arms and then slam the door in their parent's face.

Another reason why some Christians don't place a very high value on caring for the environment, is because the Bible tells us there is a time coming, when (because of mankind's sins) God will destroy the earth with fire, and create a new, perfect earth.[28] Since many of the "last days" prophecies are being fulfilled now, some Christians are thinking that since we don't have much time left on this earth, we should really be focusing on living for the things of eternity (helping to bring other

---

[26] Romans 1:22-25
[27] Romans 1:21
[28] 2 Peter 3:13; Revelation 21:1

people to Heaven, etc.) and not focusing too much on the temporary things on this earth.

Is the God of the Bible sexist?
(Why does the Bible call God, "He"?)

"God is Spirit."[29] Since God is Spirit, God is not what we would commonly think of as "male" or "female." In fact, the Bible tells us, "God is not a man..." (a human being).[30] God is not a sexual being, nor is "He" a biological male. In the Book of Genesis, we are told, "God created man in His own image; in the image of God He created him; male and female He created them."[31]

We see from this verse that all people are created in the image of God- and we are created male and female. So, both men and women are created in the image of God. Men are not in any way superior to women. Nowhere does the Bible say or imply that men are better, smarter or more spiritual than women. Women and men are both created in the image of God.

There are a number of verses in the Bible where the more feminine characteristics of God are revealed. "As the eyes of a maid to the hand of her mistress, so our eyes look to the LORD our God."[32] And God says, "Now I will cry like a woman in labor..."[33] and "How often I wanted to gather your children together, as a hen gathers her chicks under her wings."[34]

In fact, Jesus was considered a revolutionary in the way He treated women. While they were considered by many in the culture of Jesus' day, to be second class

---

[29] John 4:24
[30] Numbers 23:19
[31] Genesis 1:27
[32] Psalm 123:2
[33] Isaiah 42:14
[34] Matthew 27:37

citizens, Jesus stood up for women and gave them honor.

So, why does the Bible refer to God as "He" and "Father" etc.? God contains all the qualities of both male and female genders, but He has chosen to present Himself with an emphasis on masculine qualities of fatherhood, protection, strength, etc. Metaphors used to describe Him in the Bible include: King, Father, Judge, Husband, Master, and the God and Father of our Lord Jesus Christ.

Since that is how God refers to Himself, that should be good enough for us.

Do Christians Hate Homosexuals?

No, unless those Christians are in sin. God loves people, but He hates sin. Christians should also love people, including homosexuals; but hate sin. The Bible clearly teaches that just as pride, selfishness, greed, strong sexual desires (other than for one's own spouse), gossip, slander, stealing and other things are sins; so is homosexuality.[35] God desires for each one us to live according to how He designed us to live. God created people a certain way but because of mankind's sinful nature, we may have desires that are not pleasing to God and are not good for us.

It is often the case that we don't choose our attractions. Someone may feel like they have an orientation toward lying, anger, lust, gossip or homosexuality, but that doesn't mean those behaviors are therefore ok with God, or good for us. But God understands and cares. And God is able to help us to resist temptation, no matter how strong the temptation is. In fact, resisting the temptation to sin may be the

---

[35] Genesis 1:26-27; Leviticus 18:22-30; Jude 7; Romans 1:26-27,32; 1 Timothy 1:9-10; 1 Corinthians 6:9-11

most difficult struggle we will face in our lives,[36] but God wants to help us to live in ways that are pleasing to Him and good for us. That's one of the things about receiving Jesus as your Lord and Savior- the power of God's Holy Spirit comes into your life and you are able to resist temptation.[37]

Back to the point of Christians hating homosexuals; it is a very sad thing that some ill-informed and immature Christians, as well as many so-called "Christians" do hold hatred in their hearts toward homosexuals. Those people are not following Christ in that attitude. Jesus died to pay the penalty for every sin- including homosexuality. Every Christian should love homosexuals, and as far as I'm aware of, all of the Christians I know, do love homosexuals.

What's Next?

God gave every one of us life. He is love, and He wants every one of us to know Him personally. He has a wonderful plan for your future. If you don't know for certain that you know God personally, I encourage you to talk to God. Ask Him to reveal Himself to you. Why not conduct that grand experiment that I conducted 30 years ago. Pray something like this, "Jesus, if you are real, please come into my life and forgive my sins." And start to talk to Him. He will hear you. Then watch and see what happens. Be open and look to see how God will answer your prayer and reveal Himself to you. He loves you.

Or better yet, why not surrender yourself to God right now, and receive Jesus as your Lord and Savior. Decide to turn to God and pray something like this, "Dear God, Please forgive me for my sins. Jesus, Thank you for suffering and dying on the cross for my sins.

---

[36] Hebrews 12:4 (NASB)
[37] 1 Corinthians 10:13

Please come into my life and be my Lord and Savior. Help me to follow You. In Jesus' Name I pray, Amen."

If you have questions about God or want to grow in your relationship with God, you might want to check out www.allaboutGod.com, and it would be very helpful for you to go to a Bible-believing, Bible-teaching church. People say a lot of things about Christians and about God. Instead of forming your opinions from second and third hand accounts, why not go find out for yourself?

Jesus loves you.

Appendix

The Reed in the Wind

In the third chapter of this book, I shared about the reed that stood straight up in front of me. I shared about how the message shot through me; that when I was about 40 years old, I would be connected to a multitude of people and that the spiritual force that connected us was going to "move mountains."

You might wonder if anything, happened to fulfill the "prophecy" that I believe God gave me. Well, when I was 40 years old, my wife and I were serving with a mission organization in Texas. The organization trained and sent out thousands of Indian pastors in India who were telling people the Good News about Jesus and the God of the Bible.

At the time, about 80% of the people in India claimed to be Hindus. Because of the teachings of Hinduism, some (possibly as many as 300 million) people are called Dalits and are considered to be "untouchables." (If a high caste person touches one of them, the high caste person considers themselves to be defiled.) Hinduism teaches that due to deeds they have done in past lives, Dalits have been born in this life to suffer in order to pay off their karma (retribution for past life deeds).

While the caste system is illegal according to the Indian Constitution (and many high-caste Indians in the US don't believe that the caste system is still operating in India), in the rural areas (where about 75% of India's population lives) it is still widely practiced and entrenched. Dalits are often desperately poor and assigned the worst and dirtiest jobs available- from street sweepers to latrine clearers and mortuary workers forced to handle dead bodies. Millions of Dalit women have been raped. Dalits are often treated worse than animals and practically live as slaves of the upper-caste Indians.

As a result, many Dalits live hopeless lives. But the message has been getting out to the Dalits that they are not "untouchable," that all people are created equal in God's eyes, and that God loves them and sent His only begotten Son to suffer and die for their sins. As you can imagine, believing that your entire life is being lived to suffer to pay the penalty for past life sins (bad karma), and then hearing the truth that the God who created the universe, loves you and sent His Son to suffer and die for you, is a welcomed message of love and hope for so many.

While I was serving in the ministry in Texas, we were praying for a large meeting of (reportedly) 100,000 Dalits (including many Dalit leaders) that occurred in Delhi in November of 2001, where Dalits were being told about (among other things) the love of God. Within a year or two of my turning 40, hundreds of thousands of Dalits heard about the love and truth of God and since that time, millions of Dalits have heard the Good News and many have turned to Christ. In the same way that millions of people in China and Africa have become followers of Christ in recent years, God is "moving mountains" in India and multitudes are receiving the joy, peace and certain hope of Heaven that only a relationship with Jesus Christ can give- the same joy, peace and certain hope of Heaven that God wants you to have.

Thank you for reading this book.

If you were blessed by this book, please consider leaving a positive review on amazon.com and/or bn.com. And if you decided to ask Jesus into your life after reading this book, we'd love to hear about it and to send you a free New Testament of the Bible if you'd like to receive one. Feel free to email us at: contact@firstcallpublishing.org

God bless you.

OTHER BOOKS BY STRAT GOODHUE-

HOW TO KNOW THE WILL OF GOD

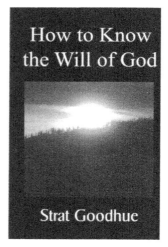

What's worth more than all the riches in the world?

The deep, lasting peace and sure confidence in the future that comes from knowing you are walking in the will of God. How do you know when God is leading you? Get this book and find out. 190 pages.

THE PLACE OF JOY

What does every one of us long for?

Joy- the rich and lasting joy that comes only from the Living God. God wants to give us "fullness of joy" and wants to take ordinary people and bring us to a place of extraordinary joy. Find out how. 236 pages.

Order copies for $9.00 ($7.00 for *A Different Life*) on amazon.com, bn.com or by calling us at: (425) 577-1469. Bulk order discounts available.

Made in the USA
Monee, IL
18 July 2021